KILENGE LIFE AND ART

KILENGE LIFE AND ART
A look at a New Guinea People

PHILIP J. C. DARK

ACADEMY EDITIONS · LONDON
ST. MARTIN'S PRESS · NEW YORK

First published in Great Britain in 1974 by Academy Editions 7 Holland Street London W8

Copyright © 1974 by Academy Editions. All rights reserved

SBN 85670 011 8

First published in the U.S.A. in 1974 by St. Martin's Press Inc. 175 Fifth Avenue New York N.Y. 10010

Library of Congress Catalog Card Number 73–91220

Printed and bound in Great Britain at The Pitman Press, Bath

Contents

Preface   7

Introduction to New Guinea and
    the Kilenge   9

The Daily Round   13

Masks   16

Art and Artist   19

Canoes and Fishing   21

The Kilenge and their Neighbours   24

Across the Dampier Strait   27

Change from Without   31

Some Melanesian Pidgin Terms   33

References   33

Dates of Photographs   33

Notes to Illustrations   35

Illustrations   49

Preface

In the short essay which follows, I have tried to convey to the reader some of the more personal impressions I obtained in the course of a stay in New Guinea among a charming but little known people, the Kilenge, living on the western tip of the island of New Britain. I went to New Guinea with my colleague, Joel Maring, an anthropologist and linguist. The purpose of our visit was to survey certain areas in order to find one or two cultures where art and language and the relationship of the two, and their integration in culture, could be studied. It was hoped to return, subsequently, to make a study in depth over a period longer than was available to us in the summer of 1964 and this I have fortunately been able to do. Thus the account given in the following pages, while based primarily on my 1964 visit, is tempered by what I learned during a stay of nearly a year with my wife among the Kilenge in 1966-7, when we were joined by our colleague, Professor Gerbrands, in 1967, and in a brief visit in 1970. The text is meant to be of an introductory nature—a first look at the Kilenge—just as our first visit was in 1964, but it is supported by photographs which I took on all three field trips, for it was only on the subsequent visits that I could obtain the visual data illustrative of what I learned in the course of that first visit. A key to the dates of the photographs is given on page 33.

Our 1964 visit was made possible through grants-in-aid from the National Institute of Mental Health, Maryland, and Southern Illinois University at Carbondale; that of 1966-7 was supported by the National Science Foundation, Washington, D.C., and Southern Illinois University at Carbondale, which also helped my third visit. My thanks are due to these institutions as also to Joel Maring for his comments on an earlier draft of this essay. I would like to note with special appreciation the kindness on my first visit of the Administration of the Territory through its officers, of Mr. Ross Kelly, Patrol Officer, Cape Gloucester, of Father McSweeney and the Catholic Mission at Kilenge, of Father Sassi at Mandok, the Reverend and Mrs. Nagel at Lab-Lab, and Dr. Bettison, head of the New Guinea Research Unit of the Australian National University. On subsequent visits kindness and help were tendered both by the Administration, particularly by Mr. and Mrs. Ross Kelly and Mr. McKinnon, and the Sister and Fathers-in-charge of the Catholic Mission, Kilenge.

Permission for me to photograph a number of specimens which are reproduced in the plates is herewith gratefully accorded to the Rautenstrauch-Joest Museum, Cologne, the Museum für Völkerkunde und Schweizerisches Museum für Volkskunde, Basel, the Rijksmuseum voor Volkenkunde, Leiden, the Evangelisch Lutheraner Missionsanstalt, Neundettelsau, and the Völkerkundeliches Museum der vereinigten evangelischen Mission, Wuppertal. All photographs are by the author except illustration 90 which is reproduced by courtesy of Field Museum of Natural History, Chicago. A number of the plates included in this book were originally in colour. They were included as colour prints in *An Exhibition of Photographs of a New Guinea People* by Philip J. C. Dark. Permission to use information included in the catalogue to the exhibition, which I wrote (1971), has kindly been given by Dr. B. Hedrick, the Director of the University Museum, Southern Illinois University at Carbondale, which prepared and circulated the exhibition.

Though placed last here, foremost and above all, my thanks must go to the Kilenge people and to others of the northern coast of New Britain, and also to the Siassi Islanders among whom we intruded. I feel very appreciative of being allowed to photograph so freely among the Kilenge, who, in fact, encouraged this aspect of one's activities by sometimes arranging things so that one could make appropriate visual documentation. Particularly do I appreciate being able to reproduce photographs of the carved and painted masks, called *nausung* (see *ills.* 76-85, 118-120), for it is strictly forbidden for women to see these masks. Knowing this, I asked, when I visited Kilenge in December, 1970, whether I could include photographs of them in a book and was assured that it was all right for me to show the masks as pictures, for that was different from people seeing the real thing in the village.

Of the many Kilenge who gave their time and friendship, I wish to note Mr. Aisapo, Talania, Ailama and Namongo, all of Ongaia, Nake of Portne, Talania of Kurvok, Talania of Ulumaiinge and particularly Mr. Tule of Ongaia. With the change to a system of local government, in 1967, Mr. Aisapo ceased to be paramount chief and was elected a Councillor. Change in New Guinea has been occurring apace recently and the Kilenge have been experiencing something of it. It is a mark of their friendliness, however, that when I visited them again briefly in 1970, after a great welcome, it was as though I hadn't been away at all.

P.J.C.D.,
Carbondale, Illinois.

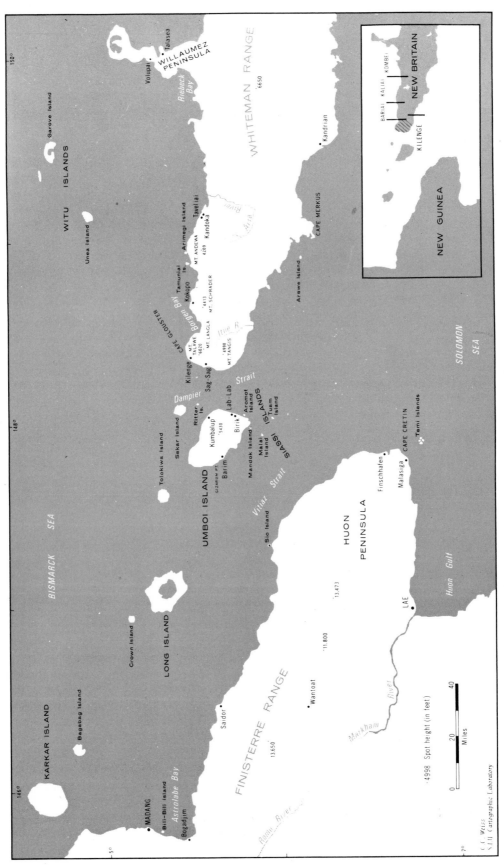

Map of Huon Peninsula, West New Britain and the Kilenge Division.
Territory of Papua and New Guinea.

Introduction to New Guinea and the Kilenge

The Island of New Britain is part of the Territory of Papua and New Guinea, which is administered by Australia as a Trust Territory of the United Nations. The term New Guinea is used to refer to the island of New Guinea, thus including West Irian and Papua and New Guinea. The term is commonly used to refer to the territory of Papua and New Guinea, including the large islands of the Bismark archipelago to the east, of which New Britain is the largest, with an area of 14,000 square miles. Rabaul, the capital city of New Britain, is located at its eastern end. Ships from different parts of the world call at Rabaul but few do so regularly. Thus it is easier to visit New Britain, and New Guinea, by plane, for there are daily services between Australia and New Guinea and, within the Territory, flights are regular to many parts.

The overseas traveller starts his flight north from Sydney. The plane I took was a DC-6.[1] It left every evening about nine o'clock and, with one stop at Brisbane, reached Port Moresby, 1830 miles away, at about six o'clock the following morning. Except for the lights of Sydney to port, as the plane swung northward, and the gloom of a bare, inhospitable hangar at Brisbane in the early hours of the morning, there was nothing to see. It was only on the return flight, which took place in the daytime, that the magnificent panorama of the Queensland coast and of the Great Barrier Reef could be enjoyed. Much of the Queensland coast seemed like a giant Rorschach test, for rivers and inlets twisted and twined among the sands, spreading out like blots on brown paper. Stretching to the west into the purpling haze was an apparent empty wilderness, suggesting that if one traversed it one would close with the dim and distant past of the beginnings of the earth.

At Port Moresby, the plane paused for some forty minutes before proceeding on its way north and east across high mountains to Lae on the eastern shore. Port Moresby is the administrative centre of Papua and New Guinea. It is located on the south coast of the island of New Guinea, in Papua, inconveniently remote from the rest of the Territory though convenient as a funnel of routes from within to outside Australia to the south. At Port Moresby is the new House of Assembly, insuring representation of the people and the right to run their own affairs. But most of them live in the country remote from the centre and know nothing of the affairs of the world outside their local hearth, let alone outside New Guinea. They are aware of the aeroplane, for it is often the means of communication with the larger world of the Territory beyond their homes. The innovations of Western man, such as iron axes, Tilley lamps, soap, matches, tobacco and corned beef, reach remote parts and are accepted as useful and as an im-

[1] A jet service from Australia to Port Moresby was initiated in 1967. It cuts down considerably the flying time and tediousness of the journey north and south. Fokker Friendships fly between Port Moresby and Lae.

provement on traditional ways of living. The city attracts the young. Schooling, provided by the government and missionaries, who must outnumber the government in officers, gives a young man or woman the opportunity to seek the city and make money to return home and establish himself and a family. But once away from home, many stay in the city where the types of problems common to urban life in all parts of the world are developing. Happily, the spreading of news and culture is restricted to newspapers and the radio, and the radio service is not yet dependent on commercial advertising for financing. But how long will it be before New Guinea really adjusts to the inevitable, permeating pattern of Western culture and enjoys the benefits of television and the insistence of Western advertising that the only way to live is to defend yourself against pain and odour and go through life without a blemish?

The traveller, who has never before visited New Guinea, will initially be swept into a world of stimuli deriving from such fresh impressions that he will not pause to consider anything but the novelty of contact with mountain and river, forest and sea, so different from any previous experience. Only after a while, if he stays, will he begin to philosophize on the fate held in store for the charming and friendly peoples he encounters in a unique corner of this world.

It is not until the plane leaves Port Moresby that excitement and pleasure at the 'discovery' of a new land will really stir the traveller from the lethargy and regimen of international air transportation. Certainly the humidity, if not the heat, will strike him while he waits at Moresby for the plane to take off again. But any discomfiture felt will soon be lost as he passes over the serpentine courses of the Brown and Vanapa rivers, while the plane climbs steadily to negotiate the Owen Stanley Range, which forms part of the high mountains, stretching east and west along the central spine of New Guinea. After a quarter of an hour or so, the plane starts to cut through the valleys scouring the mountainous landscape of the Highlands. In breaks in the clouds, a deep valley, with a faint white fleck of foam from a waterfall, can be seen far below. The next minute the tip of a wing almost brushes the top of a razor-edged escarpment and you feel as though you could lean out and touch the tops of the trees clinging precariously to its precipitous sides. For everywhere are trees. Only the river courses and the hand of man show that there are rocks and soil and substance, that New Guinea is not a great green raft afloat in the Pacific Ocean.

In the face of the tropical virulence of nature, the stretch of man's hand is puny, but, though puny, it can be remarkable against the power of natural growth. In the New Guinea Highlands man is still, in many parts, dependent on the simplest of tools with which to combat the ever-encroaching flora and grow the crops of yam or taro basic to his wresting a subsistence from the land. As one flies over the thick, green carpet of trees, penetrating a cloud, clearing a mountainous edge or skirting a rocky outcropping, every now and again one can see that the hand of man, like the jaws of a moth, has left its impress on the green pile below: a slight scar on the side of a hill, with one or two huts neighbouring a small clearing; or, perched precariously on the edge of a ridge, can be seen a hamlet of a few dwellings with a path running along the razor edge to a shelf where a few more are similarly placed; slashes in the green forest, on either side of the precipitous slopes of a valley, bear witness to his activities as horticulturist. Down below it is cold, for some people in New Guinea live at 6,000 to 7,000 feet; blue smoke, permeating the green, signals habitation and life.

The plane suddenly ceases to climb over the mountainous spine of New Guinea. It leaves the clouds and comes out over the Huon Gulf. With Parsee Point astern it turns north towards the northern shores of the Gulf. To port, the Markham Valley comes into focus and the specks of settlement of Lae. Losing height gradually, the sea begins to focus and one becomes just that little bit more caught in anticipation of the experience of dropping on to the edge of *terra firma* as it meets the rippling and unstable sea. At the end of the runway at Lae, in the shallows, is a rusting wreck, legacy of the second World War and reminder that the Japanese occupied the town. Lae was largely destroyed, but a new town has been built and it is the centre of communication for the Territory. People come out of the bush for a few days of relative luxury in Lae. From Lae, after a tour of duty in a small town or post in the interior, people take the plane south to Australia and civilization. Or, with briefcase, they may be in transit from Moresby to some other part requiring inspection or investigation. A few wear trousers, shirts and ties but most wear long socks, shorts and open shirt. However, not all those who bustle round airports such as at Lae are of European extraction, for the people of New Guinea themselves are using the Western convenience of air transport. Frequent passengers will be a native police constable and his family, on transfer.

Lae is the departure point for New Britain but it was chance that led me to choose New Britain as a place where an art, still largely traditional and free of Western influence, could be studied. New Guinea is known to be one of the few lands where forms of what it has become customary to call primitive art are still produced in a traditional manner to function in the society of the people producing them. Admittedly, the New Guinea artist in many areas has either abandoned his role or taken on that of a tourist artist. Nevertheless, there remain one or two areas in New Guinea which are still unexplored and others which are relatively untouched by currents of Western civilization. It was felt that, if a suitable, relatively untouched people, actively producing art, could be located, it would be possible to study their art and language and determine the domains of each, the nature of their artistic symbolism and how art functioned in their culture. For it will not be long before the study of the artistic heritage of the 'primitive' artist will be entirely a study of the specimens which fill our museums. We shall certainly be able to enjoy that rich heritage and

the inventiveness of its makers from the specimens surviving to us, but we shall frequently have no knowledge of the nature of the symbolism employed or the meaning of art in the lives of the people who produced it. Do peoples of other cultures appreciate things in the same way we do or for similar reasons? Do other people mean by art the same things we do? Are there universal canons of aptness, taste and skill applicable to all arts? Such questions can only be answered by studying different living arts and comparing them to see what they hold in common.

I had first thought to venture into certain areas of the vast Sepik District which are still poorly known or not known at all. Enquiries in Moresby gave no concrete leads so I decided to go to Maprik with the idea of pushing west and west-northwest in the hope of finding a suitable culture to study. But on the eve of my departure Mr. David Goodyear, a government officer,[2] familiar with western New Britain, showed me a few, mildewing kodachromes of masks and house posts which he had seen in western New Britain. Here was an exciting art form, which was apparently still being produced and about which nothing was known. It seemed at least worth a look, so I changed plans accordingly, visiting Maprik, the Mecca of living, New Guinea art forms, for only one week.

My colleague, Joel Maring, an anthropologist and linguist, had gone to Ibadan, Nigeria, for a conference; he then flew on eastward, finally joining me in Lae. We spent three days assembling supplies, which ranged from camp beds and mosquito nets to food, fuel, light and film, and all the many domestic items necessary for living in the bush with no shop or store at hand. All our supplies would have to be flown in with us, for the only means of getting to western New Britain is by plane. Once a week Trans Australian Airways flew a DC-3 to Rabaul which stopped on the way at the remote outposts in New Britain of Kandrian, Talasea, Cape Hoskins and Jacquinot Bay.[3] Once a week the plane made a return flight. On request, when the seasons are clement, the plane will call at Cape Gloucester, on the north shore of the western tip of New Britain. At Cape Gloucester is an air strip laid down by the Japanese in World War II and improved by the Americans after they had driven out the Japanese.

Transport from the hotel to the airport was in a school bus, a ramshackled affair driven by a diminutive old man with bare feet, for TAA's airport bus had broken down. Lae airport required as much hanging around and provided as many delays as any other airport. It was just as difficult, too, to understand what was being said over the loudspeaker system as in other places. We were concerned that our rather extensive cargo should be put on board and watched anxiously as it was loaded into the front and stern cargo spaces of the DC-3. We left an hour after scheduled departure and flew along the coast to Finschhafen. After a stop there, we took off across the sea and across the Dampier Strait on the thirty-five minute run to Cape Gloucester. To port were to be seen the Siassi Islands: the inhabited islands of Tuam and Malai well to the south of Umboi, the large island, and one or two uninhabited coral

[2] My special thanks are due to Mr. Goodyear, and to Mr. Claringbold, Director of Commerce and Industries.

[3] Now a different service with a De Havilland Otter prevails.

reefs, brown rings with a shading of light blue, pushing through the dark waters of the sea. The islands below us looked beautiful and inviting in the sun. But some of the worst weather in the world prevails in these waters, as we were to learn later, and the beauty of the sea goes hand in hand with its sudden, scudding rage and storm, blackness and death. Clouds at first obscured the volcanic mountains of New Britain, but then the western coastline showed through as we followed it up from Sag-Sag with Mount Talawe to starboard, its peak lost in the clouds. Soon the five Kilenge villages, which were to be our home, came into view, nestling on the edge of the shore. The plane cut inland, passing to the north of Mount Langila, an active, volcanic cone, smoking away; stretching down its slopes are ridges of lava covered with fresh grass and bare of trees. In stream beds running to the sea are many rocks and boulders which it has disgorged. It is a barren land, indicative of violence, uninviting and intimidating. The air-strip is in the middle of nowhere; there is no tree cover. A blasting heat hits you as you step out of the plane. Most captains seem to fidget here, anxious to get off again.

Our plane came in well, though there are nasty cross currents of wind to contend with. We were greeted by Mr. Huon, the Medical Assistant, stationed at Cape Gloucester, and by Father McSweeney, the priest in charge of the Catholic Mission at Kilenge. Our gear was unloaded and we discovered, in spite of our careful watch on loading operations at Lae, that certain vital items had been off-loaded as the plane's cargo schedule would not allow it to carry all our cargo. Beds, chairs, kerosene and lamp were among the items sitting in Lae. I complained to the purser and to the pilot; the latter expressed his sympathy but remarked that he was only operational and that it was nothing to do with him. The purser promised to have our missing cargo put on the Saturday plane. The door slammed and, in a cloud of dust from the revving engines, the plane took off, no doubt with relief at having got rid of us. Mr. Huon turned out to be a Frenchman, so I reverted to his native tongue. In his second or third sentence he announced that he was a Membre de la Société des Océanistes, but as I am too, it was 'set all'. He then proceeded to inform us that the volcano was fairly active, hence the Patrol Post had been placed twelve miles to the east of the air-strip, as the 'parrot' flies, well away from fallout. Kilenge, we learned, was six miles to the west, but sheltered by Mount Talawe, which was no longer active. To encourage us, no doubt, Huon announced that he only had thirty cases of leprosy in the village, meaning Kilenge, where we were to stay. Further, a crocodile hunter had been skinning crocodiles in the *haus kiap*, the bush rest house, which was to be our home. John Huon thus rapidly gained the next two sets for the match. The blasting heat added to our wonderment at what conditions we really were going to encounter in this remote corner of the world.

Our gear was loaded onto the Administration's rather decrepit Land Rover and about eight people piled on board. After negotiating three streams, we emerged on to a black, sandy beach to allow McSweeney to embark in his dinghy to row out to the Leo, the mission launch, which was at anchor off-shore, and to proceed back to Kilenge in comfort. We continued our jolting ride along the beach and then, by means of a track, through the bush till we reached Ulumaiinge (1) and Waremo, which are contiguous and form the largest of the Kilenge villages. We passed along the main path of the village; on either side were houses on piles with plaited walls of split bamboo and palm thatched roofs. The houses to our right stood a few feet above the high water mark; those to our left nestled against the bush. Leaving Ulumaiinge, we passed a graveyard on our left (3), and traversed some three or four hundred yards of bush before reaching the next village (2). Passing over a rickety, plank bridge, we entered Ongaia, which was laid out in a similar manner to the other two villages. After Ongaia we came to a clearing with tall high palms and pulled up in front of the *haus kiap*, the government rest-house for Kilenge. Such houses are maintained in all villages in New Guinea. Climbing up the ladder into the rickety house on stilts, we soon discovered evidence of the crocodile hunter's activities and also floor boards of varying degrees of unreliability; we gradually learned, however, to avoid those which were loose and natural, Sennett-comedy traps. Watched by many eyes, we unloaded our cargo and checked to see what had been off-loaded at Lae. Mr. Aisapo, the *waitpus*, or paramount chief for the Kilenge district, came over from his village of Ongaia and had the hut swept and an ancient table produced. McSweeney came ashore from his launch (4) and we proceeded up the path with him for half a mile inland to to the mission where the ice-cold beer he produced did much to restore the *status quo*.

From the very beginning we found the people of Kilenge most friendly and charming. Our first evening, after a supper of soup, a gang of small boys came and sat with us, some on the small veranda of our house, the others perched precariously on the floor poles which stuck out beyond the veranda, and we persuaded them to sing a song. First, they gave us one in English, which they had learned at the mission school, and then another in Kilenge. Joel made a tape recording and they listened with rapt attention to the play-back, applauding themselves with great glee at the end. The following night they came to sing again, but this time with Mr. Ailama, the keeper of the cooperative store, who accompanied them, within a rather limited range of notes, on his guitar. These two episodes, of song and recording, did much, I think, to establish rapport. They certainly placed us in a strong position to record subsequently *singsings*, or dances, and speech. It was not that the people were unfamiliar with the radio, for the Kilenge school teacher had one, and there was one at the mission, but there was a touch of tension, of expectation, when the machine was recording; and then, when the play-back came, fascination, smiles, but some amazement; the feel of magic gave way to laughter, thigh slapping and some ribaldry, probably, when the end came.

Without the good Father McSweeney that first night, our spirits would have been at a low ebb. He helped us out with the loan of all the things that TAA had managed to off-load at Lae. Thus we slept on an iron bed, albeit one of iron hardness meant to mortify the flesh, no doubt, though alleviated somewhat by a mattress. He provided us with kerosene and a lamp so that we were able to see and to use our primus to heat the soup. And the following evening we discovered that the Sisters baked bread at the mission so that we were able to dispense with the hard tack we had brought with us, which would quite probably have broken a tooth after a while; few things have I eaten which were more tasteless, obstinate and impenetrable, and deserving of its name.

The first night's sleep did not come quickly. Inside could be heard the rustling of rats in the eaves and the sound of their explorations of the food containers we had left out but covered. How big were they? What tracks did they take around the room? A torch shone through the mosquito net revealed no gleaming eyes. Outside the noises of the night quite excelled any modern composer's score: one frog, (or bird?), made a noise like a shunting engine struggling up a hill after an easy passage along the flat; another sounded like the twanging of a rubber band which occasionally breaks; yet another like a water tap dripping; other sounds, strangely analogous to the machinery of our modern technological world, added to the cacaphony, punctuated by a variety of frog croaks, yacs and yaws; and suddenly all was still, and somebody started sawing wood but it was only another soloist frog in another movement of a composition which lasted the greater part of the night while the rats gamboled and we snored, intermittently.

Under the direction of the *waitpus*, a man called Nake attached himself to us, to look after our wants, so it was said. Nake was a Siassi man, from Kumbalap on Umboi Island, who had married a Kilenge girl and who had settled in the village of Portne. During the war he had worked with the Americans and had been around; he would know our needs. Our first need was to get some clothes washed. Armed with a bucket, a cake of soap and our dirty clothes, away went Nake, that first morning, with a military bustle and haste that gave us confidence. After half an hour, he came running back to say he had used up the cake of soap. We remonstrated with him and explained that we were not a soap factory, that, in fact, we had a limited supply and suggested that he use half a cake of soap in a bucket of water, leaving our clothes to soak a while; he retorted that there was plenty of soap in the village store, in fact better soap. True, there was soap in the village store, and matches, a few tins of corned beef and a mosquito net, but little else. Nake was evidently a character and turned out so to be; he was also quite evidently regarded as one by his fellow villagers, though shown some respect, partly for his having travelled but also for his ability as an artist which we were to discover; as a painter his capabilities far excelled his performance as a gentleman's gentleman. In the latter role he could never be found when wanted; in the former, once introduced to drawing with marking inks, we could never get rid of him, or stop him, till he had used up our supply and we had to have more flown in from Lae.

The Daily Round

The people of the place called rather generally Kilenge, numbering some 750 persons,[4] live in five villages on the northwestern tip of western New Britain (see map). The five villages are situated close together, being separated by some natural feature of the landscape, usually a stream. The villages are on the seashore. Some quarter to a half mile off the shore is a reef (58), which protects the coast and also helps provide a rich marine fauna for subsistence. From the shoreline into the interior, rising up Mount Talawe, is heavy tropical forest. The people have carved out of this forest, on the volcanic slopes, gardens in which they grow a wide variety of subsistence plants.

The five Kilenge villages, from northeast to southwest, Waremo, Ulumaiinge (1, 3), Ongaia (2, 4, 62), Kurvok (4) and Portne (4), are situated some six miles from the Cape Gloucester air strip.

To the west of Kilenge, across the Dampier Strait, can be seen Sakar Island (2), another of the Siassis, with Umboi Island to its west. It is with the dangers of the seas of this Strait that the people of west New Britain, and of the Siassi Islands, have to contend when their sailing canoes journey on a trading expedition.

Other Kilenge-speaking peoples live in western New Britain in a few coastal villages, to the east, in Borgen Bay, to the west, around the western coast to the Itne River, on the south coast, and in a few villages in the bush, the *lolo*, on the southern slopes of Mount Talawe and of Mount Langila, and in the tributary courses of the Itne River. But the world of the Kilenge-speaking peoples extends beyond this western tip of New Britain. As well as trading with the peoples of the Siassi Islands, primarily the Mandoks and Aramots, the Kilenge trade with the Kombei, who live on islands some seventy miles to the east along the north coast, and the intervening Bariai- and Kaliai-speaking peoples. Trade to the south and east along the south coast means contact with peoples seventy or more miles away, living as far as Arawe (see map). Trade or association beyond the aforementioned point is not now part of the lives of the Kilenge peoples, save contact with Rabual, through the visit of the Burns Philp steamer once every three months and of a mission supply ship, through the mission with its store and the Kilenge people who go to school or to work in Rabual. Formerly, however, contact with the Tami Islands, close by Finschhafen, and further afield to Astrolabe Bay and Madang was maintained.

The *haus kiap* in which we lived was situated in the clearing between the villages of Ongaia and Portne and some sixty yards back from the sea (5). A number of tall palms gave some shade but also provided a hazard, for, from time to time, a nut, quite capable of killing a person, would fall with a big thump on the ground. The main path

[4] This was an estimate. The 1967 census included nearly 1000, about a third of the Kilenge speaking peoples of west New Britain.

from the beach to the mission and the village gardens passed our house so that we were strategically placed to watch the coming and goings of a good percentage of the villagers, and be watched.

Following a typical day, we would get up with the sun, about 6 a.m., as the village itself stirred, and prepare ourselves for the activities to come. At about 6:45 a.m., the first school children would begin to make their way past our house, up the path to the mission in preparation for mass before school started at 8:00 a.m. Soon after 7:00, as the trickle of children continued, one or two adults would greet us as they passed on their way to their gardens. As 7:30 approached, more children, gangs of little boys and gaggles of little girls, would make their way to school. A few more adults would pass on their way to the gardens. A group of giggling teenage girls would wend their way along the path to school. Finally, in a hurry, the schoolteachers not living at the mission would pass. Before 8:00 a.m., we would have wended our way, individually or together, into one of the villages to seek out informants in order to pursue a particular line of enquiry; or roved along the beach, avoiding the canoe prows jutting over the sea lapping on the shore, to talk with whomsoever we might encounter; or to wander along the main path of one of the villages stopping to chat with those going about their everyday domestic tasks, or who were seated under the pile houses pursuing some job (6–14, 33, 37–39, 57).

The village would be relatively deserted, for the children had gone to school and many of the adult men and women would be away working in their gardens. Generally to be found at home, or close by, would be old man Marakos, too old to make the long walk to his gardens but usually busy for a while with some task and happy to instruct one about it. One morning I found him cracking some nuts and putting them in a carved bowl, which had been traded from the Siassi Islands. The nuts were Tahitian chestnuts. Another time he was weaving a basket (9), with one or two children, too young for school, watching him. If they became a nuisance he told them off sharply. When I first photographed him at work, crouching with the camera close to his hands threading the weft (10), he cackled with laughter at my craziness, for who would want to photograph an old man making a basket? Then he would take my strange posturing around him seriously. We soon learned that Marakos was considered a master artist, a *namos tame*, in fact, the master. When I had learned the correct phrase, I always addressed him, to his great delight, as *namos tame*. And he clearly was, for, though he had given up canoe-making or large scale carving, he could still carve a betel mortar and had recently painted the designs on prow and stern of a canoe. One morning, when I called by his house, he was not sitting in his usual place on the ground in the shade. I met him, shortly after, returning from supervising the construction of a cook house at the back of one of the houses in his village. He returned to show me how the work was progressing. For a real *namos tame* is a complete artist: architecture is but one creative outlet (15–21). And the best artist is the man who can make many things.

Often one or two women would be sitting with the old man and thus the opportunity arose of asking about the cicatrization marks they bore. The women are heavily marked on face, chest and back, arms and legs, with a variety of designs which they readily name (26–34). I showed them how they could see the picture I would take through the Rollei screen and, after oohs and ahs and giggles, was able to take a number of photographs. Old man Marakos was not too sure of the names of some of the designs but the women could name them straightaway. I suspected that there might be quite a differentiation between the aesthetic worlds of the women and the men.

Continuing a walk along the central path of the village, with its row of houses on either side and its trees and shrubs planted in a decorative manner, just as we might, one could expect to find one or two women sitting under their houses, keeping an eye on a young child or two and making *nagome*, shell rings, or bracelets, to be worn on the upper arm, from the trochus shell (33, 37–38). It is a long process but a significant one, for not only are shell armlets worn by the people of Kilenge themselves but they are an item of trade to peoples to the east. In exchanges to the east they receive plates of turtle shell on which they carve designs (40–54). The plates are then bent into armlets. Thin bracelets of turtle shell are also exchanged; a number of them may be worn either singly (60–61) or plaited together to form an armlet (55).

Under another house a woman might be stitching parts of a grass skirt to be worn at a *singsing* (59). As well as the main parts which hang in the front and the back, additional pieces, varying in design, are worn stuck in the belt at the back (60–61). Pieces of fibre are plaited into decorative elements worn tucked into shell bracelets. For everyday use it is the older women who continue to wear the traditional grass skirt, while the younger ones sport a simple *laplap*, or skirt, of trade cloth.

The main path of the village is of soft volcanic sand into which one sinks so that progress is somewhat laboured. Behind the row of houses, backing on the seashore, the canoes are drawn up. Some are large and meant for trading expeditions along the coast and across the Dampier Strait. Others are small and used for fishing inside the reef. Progress along the beach is also slow for it means skirting the stern of a canoe by wading into the shallows (136).

The people of the five Kilenge villages among whom we stayed seemed to gain their subsistence about equally from the sea and from the land, though they gave more time and energy to horticulture than to fishing. The sea is literally on the Kilenge doorstep. The people wash in it, clean their food in it, use it as a toilet, and the smallest of children is as much at home in it as walking or running on the land. In fact, the children are always in the sea, scrambling about on the reef which rises up as the water ebbs, or playing about in small canoes, which are generally in the last stages of repair and require continuous bailing. Both men and women fish but there is some division of labour, the women largely collecting shellfish while the men net and spear or fish with line.

By twelve noon the heat of the day descended upon all, upon the people and the animals, so that a general somnolence crept into the villages: people, dogs and pigs curled up under their houses and slept. The sea glistened so strongly that even a squinting eye would sometimes have to turn away. The reflected light was strong enough to cause severe burns to any fair skin, untanned and unprotected, that ventured on the sea in the middle of the day.

Though some might fish and others stay at home, every day, except Sunday, a good number of Kilenge would be up early and on their way to their gardens where they would spend the day working. The gardens of each of the five villages are situated on the slopes of Mount Talawe, back inland, and upwards, from the shore (62). The distance from the coast of any one village's gardens varies but the gardens of Ongaia, which we examined, were some three miles back and situated at six to seven hundred feet up the mountain slopes. It was a long climb in the heat, wending one's way along a path through the thick bush, negotiating obstacles, and climbing ever upward. It took us a good hour to arrive at the first clearing in the forest where three men were taking the first steps to prepare a garden; we sat down with relief on a huge log: we were soaking from head to foot with sweat after our climb. Felling the trees and clearing the underbrush by slash and burn methods (63) is a big task even when the main tool is an iron axe and not a stone one.

After our breather, we set off again into the bush and upward to the gardens of Ongaia. We came out into a vast clearing sloping up the side of the mountain with a central path bordered with logs left over from the clearing operation. Other logs were laid out neatly to mark the separation of one family's plot from another. Each male head of a household had his own garden. Generally, the men do the clearing and planting; the women weed and keep the gardens neat and tidy. In the Ongaia gardens I counted nineteen species of plants used for food of which taro was the principal crop. The taro was young and a few women were weeding and clearing the areas in between the plants. Taro is planted fairly far back from the sea, we were told, because the damp and coolness and richer soil of the slopes of the old volcano suit it better than when it is planted lower down. In addition to food yielding plants, the people plant shrubs purely for decorative purposes just as they do in the village along the path in front of a house or in the graveyard. I noted six different species of decorative plants in the Ongaia garden. Some of them provide leaves which the people use as additional forms of personal decoration when dressing up for a *singsing* or costuming a masquerader (e.g. 60, 165).

As well as the plants cultivated in their gardens, the Kilenge grow bananas, distinguishing over thirty different kinds, sugar cane and coconuts. The coconut palm is cropped for copra, which is sold either to the mission or, through the village cooperative, to the Burns Philp trading ship when it calls.

Pigs are an important item in the Kilenge economy but not as a staple to the diet. The pig is a status symbol and only slaughtered on certain ceremonial occasions and when *rites de passage* take place, such as at the circumcision of a boy or when the older boys take on adult status at a ceremony in which their ears are pierced and their hair shaved. Such occasions, or *singsings*, provide an opportunity for feasting, singing and dancing, and certain of them are accompanied by masked dancing, one of the principal forms of aesthetic expression of the people. Older men spend a considerable amount of time tending their pigs and looking after the pig sties, which are more fenced corrals than sties and which are located in the bush outside the villages. Wild pigs are hunted in the bush with dogs, a dangerous undertaking, we were told, and killed with spears. Wild pigs are also captured by the use of specially woven nets and then bred with domestic ones.

While the adults have been pursuing their everyday tasks, some wresting a living from the land, others from the sea, and others have been doing domestic chores or making bracelets or skirts, or building or repairing a house, the children have been absent at school so that adult work has been pursued purposefully or lackadaisically, as suited the person, but with a general quiet pervading the villages. The younger children begin to return from the mission school at about two o'clock, to be followed at three, or a little after, by the older ones. By four the village was astir again. Gangs of little boys played on the shore line; some frolicked in the sea close to shore, or paddled a small canoe. By five o'clock women were engaged in preparing the evening's meal of taro, sweet potato or shell fish. A young girl might be sent to peel the vegetables, using the sea as a convenient means for washing them and disposing of the scrapings. Some of the men were out on the lagoon in the cooling evening, fishing with a line or on the reef with a spear. Those who had gone to their gardens that day wended their weary way home through the bush, thankful, no doubt, that the walk home was downhill and not up, for the baskets and firewood the women carried on their heads were heavy.

At this time of day, if one walked along the shore in the warm shallows, one would always meet somebody taking it easy and ready to chat or some small boys, who would gather up shells, to give one, seemingly surprised at a display of interest in such commonplace things. Yet adults collect and keep just those shells we consider most beautiful, such as different kinds of conus and cowrie, and the opercula or cats' eyes prized by GIs and themselves, storing them away among their possessions. When our interest was discovered we were occasionally given one as a present and, since, I have sent different small shells by mail.

Soon after six, the sun went down in its ever-changing, ever-miraculous blaze of unique colours. Each sunset brought some new experience. One evening, a sailing canoe, from a village to the west, passed by with a southwesterly wind astern: the steersman stood silhouetted, black against the orange, setting sun. Gradually, the sky turned to red: little black figures walked along the edge of the shore, looking like puppets against the molten, red reflection from the sea. The blue smoke of cooking fires drifted from the village and hovered over the water. One or two canoes and their paddlers returning to the shore were silhouetted against the last flames of the setting sun. A stillness settled, broken only by the shouts of little boys playing on the beach, or by the bark of a dog. A little later the noise of drums was heard as a group of people in one of the villages started to hold a *singsing*. By this time we had cooked our evening meal and were sitting deciding whether to go and see what was going on or stay at home, for, most evenings, friends from one of the villages, with children of varying ages accompanying them, used to climb the steps to our veranda to visit us. These visits were, in some ways, the most important part of the day to us, for it was then that we learned much about the ways of the people and their language; they provided an opportunity to check on things seen and heard in the daytime and to lead on to new avenues of enquiry. But it was always ourselves who tired first in the evening sessions, for our Kilenge friends seemed inexhaustible and would have gone on talking into the early hours if we hadn't called a halt and bade them good night.

Masks

The Kilenge are very fond of children. While the business of caring for them seems largely to rest in the mother's hands, it is not uncommon, at the end of the day, to see a father carrying his young child in his arms, when visiting or gossiping with neighbours. I recall seeing a canoe go by with a man sitting on the platform, holding his young son in his arms, while his wife poled the canoe along through the shallows. I remarked to the men and two women standing by me on the beach that it was good for *meri* to do all the work. Both men and the women laughed at my sally. The Kilenge of both sexes enjoy a laugh and a smile always produces an answering smile. Women scold and sometimes shriek at each other; one young wife in a tantrum with her husband deliberately broke a beautiful Siassi bowl, a part of her dowry. But, on the whole, the Kilenge appear to be a happy people. So far, their troubles are largely their own. The outside world has not yet made a real dent in their culture. Though practising Catholics— everyone, or nearly everyone, goes to mass on Sundays— the old beliefs and customs still guide or prevail, certainly in the world of the adults.

One day we walked into Ongaia and found a number of men of the village sitting in the shade on the logs to sea-ward of the men's house—an area reserved solely for men and *tambu*, forbidden, to women. The men were apparently discussing the world and philosophizing on its affairs. They had got hold of a cover of Time magazine— presumably from the mission—which sported Alan Shepard floating through space. They thought he had gone to the moon, so I tried to explain that he hadn't done so yet but that man probably would go to the moon soon. On one of the covers was an advertisement picturing Polaris missiles which led me into an explanation of rockets. On another cover was a Rolls Royce jet engine and a Pan American stewardess serving two men in a clipper. What were these fellows up to? Rather tricky subjects to deal with when one was just beginning to learn Neo-Melanesian, or Melanesian Pidgin, the lingua franca of New Guinea.

Having tried to explain something of my world, Aisapo perhaps felt that we should be instructed in the rudiments of the Kilenge world, for he took us into the men's house together with Kauba and Ailama to interpret. The other men stayed outside and continued to gossip. Once inside we were joined by Galove and Keloy, the second and third men under Kauba.

Aisapo started our instruction by drawing our attention to a large stone surrounded by several smaller ones in the middle of the men's house. The stone, he explained, *save toktok*, that is, understood requests. Then, as so often happens in novel situations, we went off on an apparent tangent and discussed family lines and who one could marry and whom not. But though faced with an apparent *non sequitur*, we were moving from a discussion of lineages and ancestors to the subject of corporate ancestor, a figure responsible for making man, for making the world, the

Kilenge world, at least. Aisapo, having established his ancestor, and Kauba's, was then free, apparently, to move back before the time of his ancestors to the time of the creation. But the time of the creation, as described to us, seemed confused and the confusion may well have resulted from a superimposition of Catholic precepts about the supreme deity upon Kilenge cosmogony. Before the mission came, Kikikaiinge, the large stone before us, was just as a stone in the daytime. At night, however, Kikikaiinge, was just like a woman, like a pig, like a little boy, like a crab; apparently, he either made all the things he was like, or he represented a spirit, an essence, which permeated all these things and, assumedly, gave them life to continue in the active day while he remained passive as the stone in which form the eyes of man saw him.

When the mission came, holy water was sprinkled on Kikikaiinge, so, it is assumed, his energy or power no longer charged all creatures and nature. But it was Pora, who made the land and the sea, who created the world all by himself and who made Kikikaiinge and the ancestors of Aisapo and Kauba, and all other peoples' ancestors, so Aisapo recounted. Pora lived on the top of Mount Talawe as a man and sorely oppressed the Kilenge, for he made them work too hard. The people finally got so cross with Pora for being made to work so hard that he went away. First, he went to Australia, but he was buried by the Australians and after three suns and three nights he came alive and went to America, where he made aeroplanes and rockets, among other things. Pora's exodus occurred long before the Europeans came to Kilenge, before the Japanese came, before the Americans and before the mission.

Nobody could touch Kikikaiinge before 'it' was neutral-ized by holy water, except the chief priest and his two acolytes. Now, the stone is safe. But, in fact, Kikikaiinge will drive out sickness, as before. If a voyage is to be undertaken which may well be hazardous, a small prem-ium of food to the stone is a person's best insurance of a safe passage. Kauba was the chief intermediary between a person and Kikikaiinge.[5] Even though it is proper to go to church on Sundays it is best to insure that the Kilenge world, the world in which you have been brought up and know about, functions safely, just as we touch wood, avoid going under ladders or throw spilt salt over our shoulder. If you are going to fell a tree from the bush in order to make a canoe you should tell Kikikaiinge. If you are going to hollow out a canoe with an adze, or carve a betel mortar, a drum or mask, then you should tell Kauba, who will speak for you to Kikikaiinge.

Kauba, clearly, could be said to have a strong moral responsibility to his fellow men even if his role is largely mechanical. For a person can supplicate Kikikaiinge for his personal well-being which may well be in opposition to

[5] Kauba was the chief intermediary for the village of Ongaia. A person from another village would talk to his own intercessor and stone, before going on a voyage, not to Kikikaiinge. But such practices are of the past.

that of others. In both situations the chief priest, or his substitutes, are a person's intermediary. But Kikikaiinge represents collective well-being and if he had 'blessed' a voyage to the Siassis, through Kauba's intercession, a person is not likely to seek vengeance by supplicating Kikikaiinge to bring destruction down on the voyagers; instead, being well aware that a canoe has set off across the dangerous Strait, and that such a passage is not likely to have been undertaken without recourse to a 'blessing' from Kikikaiinge, he will have recourse to magic. If, however, the voyage ends in disaster—sometimes a canoe is lost in the Strait—and survivors return, then Kauba will use the power of Kikikaiinge to see that the person, who has worked magic, will 'fall down or a branch fall on him'.

Kikikaiinge appears to be the regulator of men's affairs and, provided a person has made the proper address with an appropriate gift to him, sanctions a person's actions, provided such actions are for the general well-being. If Aisapo, as paramount chief and thus the person responsible, in many ways, for all the peoples affairs, wants them to go to the bush on some task, he must, in theory, tell Kauba, i.e., Kikikaiinge, that they are to go or they won't do so. If he has the necessary sanction then Aisapo has the necessary redress against a recalcitrant. If he has not the necessary sanction then only his personality can dominate a position which might arise and, it seems possible, the people would divide on the basis of family ties and apparent jealousies between lineages. For some lineages claim their origins arose from their present native hearth, others are regarded as intrusive, their progenitors having come from outside one of the five villages. In fact, Aisapo has a very strong personality indeed backed by the people's belief in his power and respect for his administrative ability, knowledge and skills. In consequence, he has maintained a high degree of authority over all the Kilenge peoples.

One of the roles of art in Kilenge culture is the reification of sanctions in the form of masks. Aisapo, through Kauba as an intermediary with Kikikaiinge, can impose a *tambu* on certain activities. One evening, when returning from Ongaia, paddling happily through the shallows and watching the sun go down in the west, with the black silhouette of Sakar Island growing against the horizon, I was suddenly confronted by a tall masked figure, covered with leaves, rushing towards me in leaps and bounds, hefting a long spear in my direction (64). I stood my ground, but nervously, for this was my first sight of a Kilenge masked figure, or of a mask even out of costume, and of a spear, let alone one hefted in my direction. It was Aisapo's *tumbuan*,[6] sent round all the villages to mark the promulgation of a *tambu*, which he had placed on the gathering of all coconuts. The reason for the imposition of this *tambu* became apparent to us later in our stay, for, just before we departed the Patrol Officer, known to have been on tour in the interior, collecting the annual head tax in the *lolo*, the bush hinterland, and in neighbouring coastal villages, was due in Kilenge at the end of his tour, before returning to the patrol post at Cape Gloucester. The *tambu* was, in due course, lifted, shortly before his arrival

[6] I have used the Pidgin word for masked figure for the Kilenge will use it in ordinary conversation. Their own word is *nataptavo*.

in Kilenge, so that the people could gather up the nuts and make copra to sell for sufficient cash to pay the annual head tax of ten shillings, due from all adult males.

Little did we know, as we sat listening to Aisapo that morning in the men's house in Ongaia, that, tucked up in the dark shade of the eaves, was the dusty frame of a mask, called *bukumo*, which, when fully dressed, appeared to mark a significant rite in Kilenge society: the recognition that a youth was not longer such but a man. Other masks were made in the culture and belonged to families; they were displayed at appropriate occasions with suitable festivities: a *singsing* with accompanying slaughter of pigs, feasting and giving away of much food to accompany circumcision of young boys. But, to the best of our knowledge, for it was only chance that led to the display of this *bukumo* (112), only this one seemed to represent for all Kilenge the collective recognition of Kilenge society that boys were no longer boys but men.

Our first introduction to masks made by the Kilenge was in the course of a long tour of the villages of Kurvok and Portne which we undertook under the wing of Nausung, the *tultul*, the government appointed assistant to the village chief, or *luluai*, of Portne. As old man Nausung, who must have been seventy and who had nearly died from pneumonia earlier in the year, began to weary as he showed us around, we arrived in front of the two men's houses in Portne. We entered and sat down on a bamboo framed bed, one of a number on which the men sit or rest in the cool of the spacious hut. In the eaves of the high saddle-backed roof, as our eyes focused to the relative gloom, after the strong sunlight outside, we counted fourteen *tumbuan* masks, some wrapped up carefully. All of them were conical framed structures, made of split bamboo, covered with coconut bast on which features of a face or a purely geometric pattern were painted.

Unfortunately, during our stay, no public event requiring masked dances took place. The only mask functioning in the culture which we saw was that sent round Ongaia, Kurvok and Portne by Aisapo to impose the *tambu* against collecting coconuts and then subsequently to lift it (64). Aware that no occasion for calling out the masks was to take place, Aisapo arranged for a special display of them for our benefit. But, prior to this display, we gained an inkling of what another type of mask, a carved and painted one, looked like, when *tultul* Nausung showed us two such masks one morning. For a while we sat talking with him and two or three old men in the *ulumbolowa*, the place where some logs are piled in the shade and which is reserved for the men. On either side was a men's house. We had to talk quietly so that the women did not hear about the masks kept in the house. After a while we got up and went into the second of the men's houses to see the two masks, the generic name for which was *nausung*, the same as that of the old *tultul*. They were carved, in a rather elongated oval form and painted white, black and red (83). My first reaction was that they were very like Tami Island masks of the Huon Gulf (87, 89), and related ones (91), but with some difference in painting. As old man Nausung would not allow the masks to be taken outside in case the women saw them, I had to photograph them from the outside in the strong sun, looking into the gloom through the small entrance where Nausung and another man sat wearing them. However, the opportunity occurred later in our stay to photograph one of the masks being worn in the open when Aisapo arranged a special display of the *tumbuan* masks so that we could photograph them and record the songs sung to accompany the masqueraders. Though the special display was out of context, it did give us the opportunity to learn something of the function in the society of the framed and carved masks, the *tumbuan*, and the *nausung*.

We gathered for the special display at the *ulumbolowa* in Portne one morning. After a good bit of hanging around, Aisapo raised his powerful voice and shouted out in Kilenge for all the women of Portne to leave the village, because *tumbuan* and *nausung* were about to visit; he then repeated the words in Pidgin English. Four of the younger men then began to put on the *tumbuan* masks with their heavy cloak of leaves which hangs from the shoulders (67). While they were preparing themselves, Aisapo explained the different parts of the masks and the nature of the materials which go into their making. Then some of the men brought out their drums and started to play. The four *tumbuans* lined up and danced and the rest of the men sang in chorus (68). One of the four was *sukovilim*, the mask I had met rather abruptly rushing towards me one evening with raised spear. This he was now hefting but the other three masqueraders did not carry the dance clubs often born by the *tumbuan* (e.g. 128; cf. 121).

After several songs, old Man Nausung took an old palm frond and, walking towards the bush, beat the ground, calling for *nausung* to appear. The masked dancer came round the corner of a house and, peering to right and to left, hesitantly, approached the assembly in short nervous rushes. He then danced back and forth for a while, at one moment strutting confidently and then pausing hesitantly (76–77). He finally took a break, danced again and then was driven away.

Ceremonies involving masked dancers tend to occur in the season between February and October, we were told, when food is relatively plentiful for an accompanying feast. The *tumbuan* dance on occasions such as when the yams are brought in, when a canoe returns from a voyage to the Siassis, at Christmas, (65–66, 75), or to help celebrate a marriage. The masquerader dresses in his costume in the men's house and then parades through the village. The women are not supposed to see the *tumbuan* and so stay under their houses but by so doing in fact see the masqueraders pass. In olden times, if a woman saw a *tumbuan* then the village in which she lived would be surrounded by a pig's net and she and her husband and children would be captured and killed, and their house would be burned.

The feast for *nausung* used to occur every three to four years and was the occasion for circumcision of small boys. The boys are circumcised in the men's house, a razor or piece of broken bottle being used to cut the foreskin, which is buried in the ground in the men's house. Before western contact a piece of obsidian traded from Talasea, to the east, was used. The women must hide from *nausung* and only when he has been given food and sent away do they enjoy the feast of pig and taro which has been cooked in a stone oven. *Nausung* also appeared in order to honour the first new born male child and was thanked for blessing the parents with an offspring.

The morning passed rapidly. The affair ended with a special song created for our benefit about an American who comes to Kilenge by *balus* (airplane). We adjourned from the men's place at Portne to our house where we found all the women and children gathered in the clearing, looking thoroughly disgruntled at having been driven out of their village.

Two days before we left Kilenge, I was walking through the village of Ongaia in search of Ailama in order to check my list of all the married people of the villages and the houses that each occupied, when I met Aisapo. We chatted and then he took me into the men's house and showed me a dusty old bare frame tied up in the eaves. He said it was the frame of the mask called *bukumo*, who originated in Kilenge long before the Kilenge had *tumbuan*. While *nausung* appeared at the circumcision of a boy, *bukumo* appeared when a boy's ears were pierced and his hair was cut. The occasion called for the killing of many pigs to mark the importance of the mask, for the more pigs a man killed on a ceremonial occasion, the more his prestige was enhanced, and *bukumo* was the most important mask of all. Aisapo said he would get the people of Portne to make it up and that the next day they would have a *singsing*.

The following afternoon we went down to Portne to see the *bukumo* mask. On the way, I was wondering very much what form would be constructed on the strange frame Aisapo had shown me. We jumped across the little stream, which marks the northern edge of Kurvok, and, moving round the corner of the house of Sapure, the school teacher came face to face with an immense construction quite unlike any of the other masks we had seen. The mask was some twelve feet in diameter, like a giant disc, made up of many long canes, each with a feather at the end, radiating from a central janus mask constructed of pandanus fronds on which was an area of coconut bast, painted white and with the features of a face in black and red (113). A spotted crocodile, extending on to the forehead, formed the nose (111). The old men stood in front of the mask and sang, accompanying themselves on their drums (106). A wiry young man staggered out of the bush with a skirt of leaves he had made which he proceeded to put on around the hips, unlike the cloak of leaves worn from the shoulders by the *tumbuan* masqueraders. *Bukumo* was then lifted on to his head; two poles of the frame came down on either side of the wearer's body which he grasped with his hands to steady the great disc of the mask. The mask was worn fore and aft like a giant, cocked hat. The masked figure then walked along the village path of Kurvok and Portne to the square in Portne where the old men, with their drums, were assembled in the centre (112). *Bukumo* then walked sedately round the village square in a circle, producing a strange, bobbing, swaying motion of the vast open fan of feathers.

Many of the villagers had never seen *bukumo* before and a large crowd of people of both sexes and all ages came to see him dance. We learned that the mask had not been made for the last nine or ten years. In consequence, some of the young married men had not had their ears pierced. Times were beginning to change.

Art and Artist

Aesthetic expression among the Kilenge finds many outlets. Besides the construction of masks and the carving and painting of canoes, the planting of decorative shrubs and the making of shell armlets and of colourful skirts by the women, combs and betel mortars are carved, coconut containers are decorated with carved designs (189–192), paddles and taro spoons (199–204) are decorated by carving as are also a number of other items. Particular attention is given to the carving of the handles of drums and surrounding designs in low relief (99–110). The carver, himself, will decorate the elbow of his adze and even a fire-stick will have a pattern of incised lines on it.

Aesthetic appreciation is derived not only from the works of the artists but from plants grown in gardens, in the village and in graveyards for decorative purposes, as has been noted. In Mandok, one day, unobserved, I watched a small boy place his hands round a hibiscus blossom, not touching it. He spent several minutes regarding the brilliant red flower, changing the position of his hands every now and again, cocking his head to one side as he changed his view. As well as appreciating the beauty of shells, the men have an eye for a pretty, full bosomed young girl and the girls titivate themselves, bleaching or colouring their hair and sometimes even dyeing it magenta.

Among the Kilenge there are a number of artists in each village (e.g. 9, 24–25, 99). While recognition of a man as an artist carries with it recognition of his competence in a variety of spheres, such as carver, painter, canoe maker and house constructor, it is acknowledged that certain artists excel at certain artistic activities and not in others. Very few are considered to be pre-eminent in all the arts but old man Marakos was one and was called *namos tame*, master artist (9). However, others are also considered to be master artists, but would rank in public recognition below Marakos. 'A person becomes *namos tame* because everyone recognizes his skill.' An artist recognized as just *namos*, artist, will seek advice from a master or work under his direction. If an artist makes something for somebody he is given a present in return, but there is no stipulation or bargaining as to the nature of his reward before he commences. If the person for whom he makes something is pleased then he will receive a good present. While he is working he is provided with food and tobacco.

It is clear that recognition of skill at various activities is acknowledged in Kilenge culture, that certain people excel over others at tasks which we would consider require the application of skill and knowledge according to aesthetic canons, resulting in the production of works of art. But it seems that the term 'art', as the Kilenge appeared to use it, is much more embracive in its meaning than many people in western culture would allow, subsuming what we would categorize as aesthetic with other manifestations of the application of man's skill and taste. Nake told me, one day, that my ring and watch, the primus stove and radio, my hat, were *namos*, but in the sense, if I understood him correctly, of the idea of the object, not the thing itself, of knowing how to create or execute something '*man save i-mekim ol samting*'.

Having for some years found marking inks a rather pleasing medium for drawing, I took some with me, thinking I might use them myself and also try to get some of the artists to draw with them. I lost my set en route but fortunately managed to get a few colours in a Chinese shop in Lae. One day, when Nake came back with our washing and had hung it up on a piece of string stretched between two palm trees, he came and sat down on the veranda. Knowing he was an artist and had painted the designs on a canoe which we saw launched from Kurvok, I thought I would try to get him to use the marking inks. I showed him how they worked and that it was necessary to put a piece of paper underneath the sheet one was drawing on as the ink blotched through. I sat him down in a chair, put an old cardboard carton in front of him for a desk, gave him the sketch pad and asked him to draw (114–116). With very deep and complete concentration he proceeded to fill two pages with designs painted on canoes (116–117, 122). Nake had never handled marking inks before, but he drew with them firmly and carefully, not with sweeping strokes. His approach suggested that he wanted to be accurate and have neat lines and tidily filled in spaces. He would pause in his work, cock his head to one side, as we might, consider the whole design and sometimes go back and fill in a part of an area where he had already worked, before continuing at the point where he had left off.

After Nake had completed two canoe designs, using red, blue and green colours, I went and got my larger drawing pad in which he proceeded to draw two of the five types of *tumbuan* masks we had seen in one of the men's houses in Portne (115). I took some photographs while he was working; when he finished he asked to be photographed holding his designs and that I send him pictures of them for him to hang up in his house. The medium had apparently intrigued him, for he asked where he could get marking inks and how much did they cost.

The next day Nake dropped by the house and asked if he could take the sketch pads and inks with him to work at home. He returned later that day with two more drawings: one of a third type of mask and another of a house board carved and painted in the Siassi Islands and owned by a Mandok man living in Portne.

Introducing Nake to drawing with marking inks started something. Once started I couldn't stop him (126–127). But I was anxious to get other artists to use the medium and thus had to keep Nake's enthusiasm at bay (123–124). One evening, Ailama brought to the house Talania of Ongaia (99), who was considered a *namos tame*. Talania was quite a different personality to Nake. Nake was nervous, a fidget, a cork that bobbed on the waters of everyday life, quick to feel passing nuances and to turn them to his advantage; in fact, Nake was a bit of an operator, but, when engaged with his art, a different man, a man solely concentrating on the work developing under his hand. Talania, on the other hand, struck me as a 'deep' character; slow but considered, reserved but profound; an intellectual, who demanded of himself the exact emotion for the right artistic act. Nake was the laboured impressionist; Talania was moulded in the classic style.

Talania's approach to drawing was quite different to Nake's. First, he established the basis of the form of a mask—a carver's mask—by outlining lightly its oval shape. On this basis, holding the black marking pen lightly in his fingers, like a brush, even twiddling it, reflectively, he then set out to delineate the main forms, working in toward the centre (118–120). One had the impression that all the time he was considering the whole, not developing a linear design (78–81). His approach was that of a sculptor, who saw things in three dimensions and when faced with their two dimensional representation required an in-tellectual *volte face* to adjust to different dimensions (121, 125). Talania's reputation was that of a master carver (82).

I was fortunate to learn from the endeavours of Talania and Nake that the Kilenge observer of Kilenge works of art, knowledgeable in his subject but lacking the artist's skill, was just as sure of what the artist should represent as the artist himself. For, one evening, Mr. Tule, the *luluai* of Ongaia, was present at one of the sessions when Talania drew for me. Towards the end of the evening and towards the end of Talania's last drawing, with a rather tense air he hesitated somewhat: maybe the artist became tired. The mask he was drawing was a mask which belonged to Tule's family. And Tule knew well how that mask should look. As a result, there was considerable discussion between artist and critic as to what should be represented or not. We had reached the edge of a situation where the artist had to meet the requirements of his patron or else, presumably, his work would not be accepted.

Canoes and Fishing

Making a canoe can be quite an undertaking, particularly if it is a large seagoing one. Most families will have a small canoe for use inside the lagoon, to reach the nearby reef, and to paddle to gardens situated back from the beach some way down the coast to the southwest where the reef extends, thus sheltering the shoreline. Only a big man, however, can afford the assistance needed to make a large canoe. A suitable tree has to be located and then brought back to the village. When a big one is felled, it will be roughly hollowed out where it has fallen, in order to lighten its weight. Then, all the men and women of one village will drag it down through the bush to the beach, a task which may take them all day. The man, who is having the canoe made, has to feed all those who help. He also has to pay the *namos*, who will finish the hollowing of the canoe and shape its prow and stern and the *namos* who will paint them, as well as those who assist in assembling the platform and outrigger, and who participate at its launching.

With old Marakos, one day, I went around examining the canoes of the village of Ongaia (131–137) and learned the names of some of the designs painted on prows and sterns. The range seemed quite extensive and included representations of both land fauna and flora as well as fish; some examples are: pig's tusks, bird's wing (132, 136), a fern found in the bush (133), a type of cane from which the leaf is taken to make a woman's skirt, and a small weed found in the bush. Four types of fish form the basis of some designs, and the crab (140–141), dove and teeth of a fish are represented. The cultural significance of the representation of forms so diverse is only likely to be obtained after a very thorough study of the total culture, its ethos and rationale. We did not stay long enough at Kilenge the first time to learn in any depth how the society actually functions efficiently and provides for the general well-being and continuity of its members. One learns certain facts and gains many impressions at various levels of abstraction from the reality of individual and collective human behaviour. Initially, all is sharp and clear: one notices many things which later are ignored. The longer one lives with human beings the more individual and precise becomes one's perception of their feelings and of the nuances of their emotions, and of the significance of them. But the mere act of awareness leads to more and more conceptualization of expected behaviour, of what is accepted by the society and of what is not, of what is right and of what is wrong, for, in the day to day business of living our lives, one is guided by the familiar patterns, which are abstractions from reality and, therefore, require less effort of response. Thus, life is easier. The observer is inevitably caught in a dilemma.

As well as the Kilenge-type canoes to be found on the beaches of the five villages, I have seen both small and large canoes from the Siassis (180–182), which have been obtained in trade by the Kilenge, as well as a Manus one with two stitched washstrakes and a movable mast, made by a Manus man, a teacher at the mission school and Aisapo's son-in-law. The Kilenge may make several small canoes a year but generally not more than one or two seagoing ones. A canoe, in service, can last up to four years but much depends on whether it escapes the worm that seems inevitably to attack the hull. The big Kilenge canoe is a single outrigger with a movable mast (153). It is a fine sight to see one at sea under sail (156).

We happened to arrive in Kilenge at a time when two seagoing canoes were nearing completion. We were able to observe the final adzing of the interior of the hull (142) and the final shaping of the prow and stern before they were painted (143–145, 152). At the very last, the platform and outrigger were attached. In the case of the canoe being made in the village of Kurvok, in order to hasten the launching ceremony, old cross pieces, or booms, were used as supports for the platform, even though they were considered *siyange*, no good. They would, it was said, be replaced with new ones before the canoe did any serious sailing (145–148, 151).

The activity of launching a canoe starts with a *singsing* in the evening before the actual launching. A fire is lit on the beach close to the canoe. Several old men, stand around the fire and sing, accompanying themselves on their drums. On this particular occasion they were led either by Aisapo or old man Marakos, who would sing solo for a bar or two while accompanied by the other drummers; then all joined in chorus. To us their drumming and singing was monotonous, reminding me of some southwest Indians of the United States performing at an annual dance. The songs that were sung were old and, we were told, had not been sung for some time; they were sung so that we could record them. We had not asked the people to put on the *singsing* for us; it was their idea, typifying their response during our stay to our quest for knowledge about their customs and way of life.

A song would last for a few minutes and then would come a short pause before the leader started off again. After a series of songs the men would sit down around the fire. Sitting around them and on the canoe were a few other men and women and, further back, in the shadows, stood some young children and girls. At one point, Tom Sapure, the Kilenge schoolteacher, brought out his Coleman lamp and hung it on a beam of the temporary shelter, which had been erected over the canoe to keep the heat of the sun off the newly adzed wood and those working on it. The men started to sing and drum again and two old women, one nursing a baby, started to dance in the lamp light. They shuffled their steps back and forth, slowly weaving their hands in front of them in time with the music, singing quietly to themselves as the men sang out boldly. The men were the focus of the *singsing* but there was quite a bit of giggling from the younger women in the shadows as the two old women moved slowly back and forth.

21

The *singsing*, we were told, would continue through the night and the canoe would be launched at dawn. After making some recordings and having stayed quite a while, we decided that we would not see the night through but catch some sleep and be ready for the launching in the morning. In most situations the Kilenge have a fine *mañana* or *immer morgen*, approach to life, ignoring time as a regulator of affairs. But the launching of the canoe was an exception. With the sun just up, we walked down to the shore to see Aisapo and the old men make their weary way home, having sung and drummed all night; the canoe was already launched and on its round of visits to each of the villages to receive presents, which are distributed afterwards to those who participated in the work of making the canoe. The canoe was gaily decorated with fresh leaves hanging along its sides from thin, green bamboo poles, which had been lashed temporarily to the gunwales. A temporary mast sported small flags, and one man, standing in the stern, wore a triangular *singsing* hat (149), usually part of the costume of a dancer at *Sia* (e.g. 174). There were about twenty people perched precariously on the hull and platform of the canoe, which was almost awash from their weight. They sang to the accompaniment of two drummers. The canoe was paddled fairly rapidly to Waremo and Ulumaiinge, and we followed along the shore, meeting it on its return at Ongaia, where it put in and received a few gifts of mats and two paddles and our offering of newspaper, sticks of tobacco and twenty shillings. It then landed at the spot in Kurvok from whence it had been launched; the 'loot' was distributed and a small boy anchored the canoe to a stick in the shallows (150); the men wended their weary way to their homes to sleep off the night's festivities.

A wide variety of shellfish is gathered by the women from the reef; we found that the people had a rich vocabulary for identifying the different species garnered. Reef fishing is the business of the men, and here too the sea produces a plentiful and varied harvest of fish. Beyond, in the deep water, are many fine fish for the taking.

The men will go out at night and fish on the reef by the light of a Coleman pressure lamp, if there is one available in the village and anybody has any kerosene. Joel, a keen fisherman, went out one night with three men and our Coleman lamp—actually on loan from Father McSweeney—but lit with our kerosene. He said he saw nothing below in the black depths, but his companions managed to spear three large fish though they complained that the moon was too high and drove the big fish too deep.

It is a common sight in the daytime to see two or three women, with a couple of children sitting on the outrigger platform, setting off for the reef to gather shellfish, squid and small fry. While in the shallows they pole their way along but take up paddles on reaching deeper water. The lagoon can be fairly shallow at low water, for the reef is well exposed and the fisherman can pole his way to shore if he avoids the few patches of deep water, which provide continuous anchorage for vessels of twelve to fourteen feet draught, and perhaps more.

One day a collective fishing drive by all the men of the villages of Portne and Kurvok, took place. It was largely for our benefit but, in fact, can only be performed on the occurrence of very low water which takes place once or twice a year. For this particular occasion we were up at dawn, as instructed, but knowing full well that time was relative to impulse which actually propelled the Kilenge to function, not as premeditated. We did, in fact, get started fairly close to the previously stated time for departure. We climbed aboard a small canoe and were poled by Nake past Portne for about a mile southward towards the reef, which shelters Kilenge. After about twenty minutes under the boiling sun, we came across two or three large canoes anchored to the north of a line of nets, stretching from the shallows shoreward towards the reef and open sea. The nets had been placed the night before. There were four types of nets in the long line strung out reefward, varying with the degree of fineness of the mesh (154–155, 157–160): those with the smallest mesh were placed inshore, those with the largest towards the reef. We transferred to one of the large canoes and sat on the platform in the blazing heat, waiting for the tide to ebb. After a while we pulled up an anchor and went along the line of floats, the men spearing one or two fish; but the tide was still too full so we returned to anchor and sat patiently in the sun. After a further interval the men decided it was too hot so we went over the side and waded ashore to join the main body of fishermen, who had sensibly, long before, decided to wait in the shade of some palms. Why the emphasis on rising early when at ten a.m. the tide had still not ebbed sufficiently for spearing fish? Finally, it was decided to get underway, but before we waded out to the canoes a thorough check was made of all men present to learn whether anyone's wife was pregnant. Only Nake's wife was, so he had to remain on the shore and could enjoy the shade. Joel did not confess that his wife back in the States was expecting a baby.

After wading back to the canoes, we began to close the nets. Suddenly, great excitement and much shouting: someone had spotted a turtle. Men fell overboard, some jumped overboard, canoes crashed into each other and nearly tipped over as everyone tried to get to the turtle, which had been trapped by the tide. Somehow we managed to hang on to our cameras as a canoe bumped ours and the outrigger rose out of the water, causing the platform to tilt precariously; but by shifting our weight the outrigger went down and we gained stability. Finally, a spear found the poor creature, which was hauled aboard and held up for all to see. Men and canoes untangled themselves; the excitement died and we poled towards the nets.

At first, there was not much success. As the tide ebbed, a number of men put on goggles, which were made of plastic and secured with a rubber band—they were imported from Japan—and, floating on the surface, paddled slowly along looking for fish. A small island of coral began to appear as the sea ebbed. The men put a net round it and one of them, taking a bundle of fibres, obtained from a creeper, crushed them with blows from a stone on the prow of one of the canoes; after soaking the bundle in the water, he leant down inside the net and inserted it under the coral outcropping. The poison from the bundle killed or stunned one or two smaller fry but drove the larger fish out of their shelters in the rock towards the encircling net where they were promptly speared by the waiting fishermen.

A spear had some eight to twelve long metal points spraying outward from the base. The fisherman would take the speared fish and slip a line, cut from a stiff but pliable plant fibre, through a gill and the mouth of the fish, or toss the fish into a nearby canoe. He rarely missed, but if he did, a small boy in the canoe would lean over the side and spear it again. Quite often a fisherman would bite the back of the head of the fish before throwing it into the canoe; one fellow, to show off for a photograph, even put the whole head of the fish in his mouth.

When the men felt that all the fish which had taken refuge under the small coral island had been caught, they would move the net to another one or divide up to cover the various smaller coral outcroppings which gradually appeared as the tide ebbed. At one of them, a fisherman put on his goggles and going under water pushed the poison right under the rock. By now the water was only up to our thighs. As the tide ebbed so the long line of nets had gradually been drawn in a semicircle closer to the shore. Men from Ongaia were fishing to the south of us and they joined their line of nets with ours to form a great big arc, which was drawn gradually in towards the water's edge. The men would gather up the net and bring it shorewards, wait for ten or twenty minutes while spearing any fish that broke for the net and then move it again. There was much hanging around with occasional rushes as a man threw his spear and splashed after it to recover it. Finally, the sea had ebbed sufficiently so that it was just below our knees and the great arc of nets was close enough to the drying shoreline that it could be left untended and spearing became a free for all.

By this time it was after mid-day and Joel and I, our faces well burned by the reflection of the sun from the water, decided to call it a day. We waded ashore and walked along the beach back to our hut and sought refuge for our thirst in some warm beer. We learned later that the fishing drive had been a great success so that the inclusion of Joel, whose wife was pregnant, among the fishing party had not been detrimental to its success. However, he himself had no success except to spear a moray at which the men laughed and then threw it away.

The Kilenge and their Neighbours

Although the Kilenge are in touch with the world of aeroplane, ship, missionary and government, the most important world outside theirs, to them, is that of their neighbours to the east, west and south, where live those with whom they trade. During our short stay, visitors, from Kaliai and Bariai to the east called at Kilenge for that purpose. In July and August, sailing conditions along the north coast are good, but the weather in the Dampier Strait is bad and the people do not venture to the Siassi Islands, nor do the Mandoks and Aramots, who live there, voyage to the mainland of New Britain.

One day, seven canoes from Kaliai,[7] on their way to Sag-Sag, called at Kilenge. They anchored off what we had came to regard as 'our' beach and we wandered down to see the strangers, feeling very much that we were part of Kilenge and that we were faced with the temporary presence of foreigners. First, two canoes arrived, being poled through the shallows off the beach, although they were rigged for sail. Piled on their outrigger platforms were their belongings, which seemed to consist mainly of mats. Soon, the first two to arrive were joined by three more. The people who had disembarked either hung around, gossiping with the Kilenge, or lit fires to prepare the evening meal. Ordinarily, when one walked along the edge of the shore one could see many shells in the shallows, shells which had been gathered by the Kilenge and thrown back into the sea after their contents had been consumed. On this particular evening the people from Kaliai had soon added their own refuse to the clear waters.

As I approached the visitors, a man with a large spear and shield, and with two curved boar tusks held in his mouth (e.g. 165), pranced threateningly towards me. He wanted his photograph taken. Two other men with spears and shields joined him. The shields had fine circular designs painted on them (e.g. 158, 162–163) and one of the shields was also painted on the inside but with rather different forms.

Two of the three canoes, which had arrived late, had their prows painted. On one side of one of the canoes, Nake recognized the design of a crab, a motif the Kilenge use (141), but did not know what the other designs represented. It seemed that there was an example here of the overlapping of design domains. At least Kombei, Kaliai, Kilenge, Sag-Sag, the Siassi Islands and Madang, and Arawe, formed points on an area of trade the extent of which might coincide with a design area.

The five canoes, which had arrived, were drawn up in the shallows and made an impressive silhouette against the sun as it sank into the sea just north of Sakar Island. Our visitors were going to Sag-Sag for a *singsing* and to trade, we were told. Some were Catholics and some Seventh Day Adventists. The church at Sag-Sag is Anglican. To trade, they had brought bark mats, shields and shell money and sought carved *plet*, bowls (218–224), made in the Siassi Islands, and *sospen*, clay pots (161–162). The Siassi people get the clay pots from Madang in exchange for sago and mats, the Kilenge said.[8] The shell money (23) brought by the Kaliai, who obtain it from their immediate neighbours the Kombei, goes from Sag-Sag to the Siassi Islands, as well as the mats. The Siassi islanders use the shell money they get to buy tobacco from the Kilenge, who have a reputation for growing good leaves, and also grass skirts, which the Kilenge are said to make better than others. The Kilenge require shell money as one item of the bride price—five fathoms is a minimum—but they also use it to obtain pigs and turtle shell armlets from the Kombei peoples, when they sail to the east. The Kaliai neighbour the Kombei so that the shell money they obtain from them, after passing through many hands and over some two hundred miles of sea, returns to those who manufactured it and put it into circulation in the first instance.

On the evening of the visit of the people from Kaliai, there was a *singsing* in Ongaia. After supper, Nake appeared at our hut and we went off with him to see the excitement we could hear in the distance. A large crowd was gathered in the village street at the back of the men's house of Ongaia. A Coleman lamp hung from a beam of the veranda of a house and, nearby, two old women held up large bamboo torches. A place was made for us to stand beside Aisapo and then a small bench was brought and we sat down, one on either side of him.

The dancing was in full spate when we arrived. The performers were the visitors from Kaliai. A chorus of ten young girls shuffled in the heavy sand towards a large group of men, who stood in a crescent at the back of the men's house with their shields held in front of them in one hand and their spears held vertically in the other. One of their number was a drummer. A man would sing a few words, then the chorus of men would chant. The young girls, in their grass skirts and with bared breasts, would bend forward and do a vigorous and rapid shuffle from one foot to the other on the same spot, causing their short grass skirts at the back to bounce up and down provocatively, like a ballerina's tutu (164, 166, 168). The line of girls had their arms linked. Every now and again they would move several steps to the right and then to the left. Behind the girls, an old dame, wearing a grass skirt and keeping in step with the chorus so that her breasts flapped to and fro, would punctuate the dancing and singing with a shrill, hooting whistle. At intervals, two or three men would rush out from their crescent on each side

---

[7] The Kilenge will speak generally of the area between Bariai and Talasea as Kaliai, lumping the Kaliai and Kombei together. These canoes were probably Kombei ones though I did not, at that time, distinguish them as such during their brief visit.

[8] The pots referred to as from Madang are, in fact, made on the island of Bilibili close by Madang. A major supplier of pots is Sio Island, across the Vitiaz Strait and thus closer to the Siassis than Madang and it was, in fact, apparently on Sio that the pots seen were made.

of the chorus line, their shields held out in front of them, and brandish their spears threateningly, turn, and then return to their fellows (158, 163). The whole affair developed a monotony of a hypnotic kind. To our ears the tune was limited and the rhythm monotonous. We suspected that variations lay in the lyrics. At one point, we caught the word Sag-Sag: perhaps they were recounting their journey from Talasea and why they were going to Sag-Sag? The chorus of girls would have outdone any Western chorus line in vigour and endurance and certainly competed in looks and figure (168, 170). Every now and again there was a pause and one or two girls, their bodies glistening with perspiration in the flickering light, would break off for a short rest, missing a chorus or two (167).

The *singsing* went on well into the night but at dawn the visitors were gone on their way to Sag-Sag.

The *singsing* we saw was called *agosang*. At most Kilenge *singsings* it is the men who do the drumming and singing and the women the dancing: the participation of the men with their shields was intermittent. There is however, one cycle of *singsings* which the Kilenge perform in connection with the planting and cropping of taro which is called *sia*. Here the men are the principal performers, dancing with their drums, while the women dance on the edge of the 'stage' (169, 171–178).

Some weeks later another expedition from Kaliai to Sag-Sag called at Kilenge on its way home to the village of Kandoka. One of the visitors was a retired police sergeant, Penga, who had served for twenty-five years in the Territory's constabulary. He called at our house and asked me to come and see his sailing canoe, which was drawn up on the beach of Ongaia (179). It was a Sunday and there were many people around, for they had just come back from church. I took a number of photographs of Penga's canoe and asked him questions about the names of the different parts in his *tok ples* (his language). He had one of his men hoist the sail, even though the canoe was on the beach, so that I could see what a fine canoe she was. Aisapo came up and began to explain the various parts in Kilenge. He held out his hand and grasped the halyard to lean on it and the yard came down on his head, nearly knocked him out and cut a four-inch gash just above the left brow, laying the skin open to the bone. I was standing just beside him. I shoved my handkerchief, which was none too clean, on the gash; somebody rushed into a house close by and brought out an old cotton pad which I put on top and made him hold it in place; I then guided him along the beach and took him to the mission hospital, where the Sister, after giving him a hypo, stitched him up. I learned later that Aisapo had made Panga pay him a pound as damages for the incompetence of one of his crew for not securing the halyard properly. Penga admitted to me that it was his *liklik rong* (little fault), but I felt that, as the inquisitive ethnographer, I was somehow to blame, though in this instance I had been taken off to see something and had not been noseying around deliberately prying into other people's affairs. It was a miracle that the yard didn't fall on me too and that, in fact, it didn't kill old man Aisapo. If it had, what would have happened to future relations between Kaliai and Kilenge?

Our view of the Kilenge's outside world was further extended by a brief survey we made in the Leo east along the northern coast of New Britain as far as Kandoka in Kaliai.

Our trip was made in company with two Catholic priests, one Irish and the other German; the former's station was located among the Bariai, the nearest eastern neighbours of the Kilenge, and the latter's among the Kaliai, who lived next door to the Bariai. The Irishman we put ashore at Kokopo, the German at Taveliai, after the troubled waters had made him decline the excellent sandwiches which the Sisters of Kilenge had put up for our seventy mile trip. We enjoyed his ration.

Ashore at Taveliai, we discovered two men's houses full of *tumbuan* masks, close in style to those of Kilenge, before we repaired to higher land, back and up from the beach, where the mission was stationed and where we were kindly provided with a supper of Spanish mackerel caught from trolling astern of the Leo. Behind the two men's houses, hidden in the bush, was an enclosure where the men dressed up in their masks and costumes. The Americans had been to Taveliai: in front of one of the men's houses was a platform of old American planks. We sat on it after supper by the light of our kerosene lamp, and recorded some songs, which enabled us to negotiate the acquisition of a mask for our University Museum. Soon after we had returned back on board, the mask followed, having been carefully wrapped up so that no one could see it.

The next morning, picking our way carefully through the reefs, conned by the captain who stood right up in the bows watching the coral closely, we moved a mile or two to anchor off Kandoka, a village a little further along the coast to the east. There we found, behind the men's house, the same secret enclosure where the *tumbuan* masks were costumed. Kandoka was blessed by one or two very pretty girls and there was a lot of kidding going on between the crew about them. When we left, my field glasses were passed round to watch one of them on the beach wave good-bye. The only film I lost in the mails had a shot of Miss Kandoka in it.

Returning westward, we stopped at Tamuniai, an island off shore, close to the border of Kaliai with Bariai. Tamuniai, had been settled by Kombei peoples, the main body of whom lived to the east of Kaliai. Tamuniai could not have been more than three acres of coral atoll so that there was no room to grow anything except a few palm trees. Thus the people had to cross to the mainland in order to care for their gardens. The Kombei appeared to be fine seamen, for one of the largest seagoing canoes we had seen was drawn up on the western beach of the island.

Tamuniai might appear to represent anyone's concept of an idyllic tropical island but such islands have little to offer the people who live on them. To be sure, there are coconuts, but limited in supply according to the number of inhabitants. There are plenty of fish and shellfish on the reef, but drinking water had to be brought from the mainland, just as arduous trips have to be paid continually to the main shore in order to cultivate essential crops. Though free of mosquitoes, sand flies are a nuisance and each evening crows flock over at dusk and set up a ruckus in the trees till the sun sets. Only at dawn, each morning, do they set off singly and quietly, back to the mainland. Swimming is no pleasure, unless one enjoys swimming in a hot bath. Only the sunsets can bring awe to a man's soul, but the sun dips rapidly into the ocean and the brilliance of the stars cannot sustain reverence and pleasure through the working day. There is, however, a sense of ambivalence for the romantic, who does not live on a tropical isle but who has had a breath of its wonders, for they can so rapidly dispel the knowledge of reality. See Venus, the morning star, at a quarter to five in the morning, shining like a searchlight in the eastern heavens, its rays like the beam of the moon sparkling on the lapping sea. What is real and what but illusion?

We found that the Tamuniai had *tumbuan* and the same type of enclosure for dressing the masks as we had found at Taveliai and Kandoka. But, in addition, they had a strange, tall mask, which did not fall into the types of masks we had seen before (74). Tamuniaia thus suggested that the area of art and design with which we were concerned was limited on its eastern border by Kombei peoples (239, 240, 242), for the Tamuniai were Kombei immigrants and although they had familiar *tumbuan* masks they admitted that they had bought them from the Kilenge. The tall mask too they had obtained from the Kilenge *lolo*, the people living in the hinterland bush (75), and was not their own invention.

On our way back to Kilenge, we called at Kokopo, where we had previously deposited the Irish Father. The people of Kokopo seemed an unhappy lot and lacking the verve of the Kilenge or the Kandokans, but the impression of a short visit might well be false.

From Kokopo we sailed along the shores of Bariai and called at the Patrol Post at Cape Gloucester, the place which had held a special corner in our thinking, for it represented communication with the outside world, official communication with powers who, however remote, were there, paternally, perhaps, but also a little bit like God, for they represented finality in the conduct of men's affairs. In reality, Cape Gloucester is a small patrol post, with a small hospital and virtually nobody lives there, except the Patrol Officer and the Medical Assistant; but their presence is sufficient.

Across the Dampier Strait

Before we went to western New Britain we had made arrangements to visit the Siassi Islands, but we did not know then of the significance of the relationships between them and western New Britain. We had planned to fly, by charter, from Cape Gloucester to Lab-Lab on the east coast of Umboi Island, but the Leo, the mission launch, had to make the trip across the Strait in order that the visiting Inspector General of the order conducting missionary work in the area could visit the small mission station at Mandok Por. Father McSweeney was agreeable to our cadging a ride.

The planned starting time of the trip across was 7 a.m. Experience had taught us that we probably had little hope of getting under way at that hour. Nevertheless, we got up at 5 a.m., sent the loads we would leave behind against our return up to the mission and assembled our cargo. At 7 a.m., the two Fathers who were making the voyage actually came down from the mission ready to embark at the planned hour. But then nobody could find the captain of the Leo, so we all hung around and waited. After some while, the captain was routed out in Portne and the Leo came round from her anchorage. Our gear was ferried out in a canoe while the priests were rowed to the Leo in the dinghy. The dinghy was not left tied astern, as was the usual practice in coastal waters, but brought inboard and lashed athwartships on the stern.

We headed out to sea through the gap in the reef and then ran southward along the reef until abeam of Sag-Sag, the sea getting choppier and choppier as we moved south into the Strait. It became impossible to sit on the coach roof. Joel and the younger priest went and sat in the dinghy, with one or two of the crew, and I went below where the old missionary, the Inspector General, was ensconced in a deck chair and very much concerned with a fundamental misery of life, sea-sickness. At Sag-Sag we turned west and out into the Strait. I lay down on a side-locker, exactly amidships, and dozed most of the way across. We seemed to progress like a cork bobbing in a waterfall. It got worse and worse as we sailed across the Strait and closed the shore of Umboi Island. Waves broke right over us, landing in the dinghy on our stern, soaking Joel and the Father, who, nevertheless, preferred the fresh air to the confinement of the cabin. After four hours, all on board were relieved to make the very narrow passage in the reef at Lab-Lab and enter the shelter of a small cove. Our Kilenge crew had proved themselves fine seamen.

Joel and I disembarked, a process involving wading ashore for about a quarter of a mile. Our Catholic friends continued down the coast to Mandok Por. We climbed up to the mission, a Lutheran station, which is on the top of the cliff above the cove. Our Lutheran hosts were surprised that the Leo had not turned back. They gave us an excellent lunch of roast beef and vegetables which was a fine change from our usual diet. After lunch, with a line of

boys hefting our gear, we set off through the bush to the village of Birik, about half an hour's walk away, where there was a *haus kiap* in which we would spend the night.

Birik was a depressing place and the *haus kiap* in a poor state of repair: I put my foot through the slats which were meant to be the floor, some of which were well eaten by white ants. The roof had holes in it. It rained in the night and water poured in. We arrived in Birik on a Friday which was fortunate, for the pattern of life seemed to be that the people worked Mondays through Fridays, went to church at 7 p.m. Friday night and then, after church, had a *singsing*, dancing all night and through Saturday till 6 p.m. They then recuperated, went to church on Sunday and back to work on Monday. A very Western pattern?

Opposite the *haus kiap* was the men's house. As the evening shadows began to lengthen, I noticed a number of men preparing *tumbuan* masks and costumes for the weekend's *singsing* (70–71). The three *tumbuan* masks being got ready were in the Kilenge style. One was painted on coconut bast but, in the other two, Australian burlap from rice sacks had been used (72). The people told me that they had got the masks and the dance, which they performed that night, from Kilenge. Just at last light, three masked figures were led off down the village street, accompanied by drummers (73). Arriving at the centre of the village, the drummers started playing and the masqueraders proceeded to dance in a slow, bobbing motion in a circle around them. The weekend *singsing* was on. The women were not excluded.

After a while, in couples and arm-in-arm, their faces painted, wearing white anklets and pandanus fibre 'tutus' over freshly washed *laplaps*, with breasts covered and with a sprig of leaves in each hand, the women shuffled round the circle of drummers and chorus with a rather slow step, taking several forwards, several on the same spot and then a few paces backward. The whole performance of the women was accompanied either by a solo of a bar or two from a man, followed by the chorus, or by a rather shrieking, high-pitched solo of a bar or two from a woman, who was then joined by the other women in chorus. To us it sounded much the same as the songs we had heard at Kilenge, and from the Talasea visitors to Kilenge; it all had the same sense of monotony. I was told that the *singsing* now is but a *mélange* of bits and pieces of old songs of magic which the old men could remember, all thrown together and the meaning no longer understood.

When we left Birik the following morning, at 10 a.m., the *singsing* was still going on, but in a spiritless manner: little boys were putting on the masks and strutting into the village, trailing the now bedraggled pandanus leaf costumes in the mud left by the night's rains, which had not prevented the people from singing and dancing all night.

We had decided to go to Gizeram, on the west coast of Umboi, in order to see two anthropological colleagues working in the Siassis. The Lutheran mission has a big plantation at Gizeram and operates two launches between Gizeram and Lab-Lab, and also to service other mission activities in the islands. We boarded the smaller of the two, the Karipo, at Lab-Lab, after wading out through the shallows. The rough sea of the previous day still persisted, the wind blowing white tops off the waves in the sun. As soon as we passed through the reef we began to roll, pitch and toss about, for the seas were rolling in from the south on our port bow. It took a good hour to get into the lee of the reef on the north side of Aramot. The sun was shining, the sea blue and white-capped, as the small spot of land, providing on its less than two acres a home for about three hundred and eighty people, gradually came into view. As the island drew near, it fulfilled most people's ideas of what a tropical island should be: with its golden, sandy beach and palm trees waving in the wind. On the reef, stretching to the south of the island, some people were fishing.

As we drew into the light blue shallows on the east side of the island, one could see that every square inch of land was packed with houses built on piles. A small canoe put out from the shore and came along side expertly to take off two women passengers and two children.

We continued our journey, threading our way through the reefs, and passed between the islands of Mandok and Mandok Por. On the latter is a small mission station where we were to stay the following week. Anchored off the lee shore was the Leo, for the two companions of our crossing of the Strait were staying at the mission.

As we left Mandok and the shelter of the reef, we moved into the swell rolling up from the southwest. For the next three hours we rode the waves coming in on our port quarter. The sun flashed a brief appearance and left a rainbow to light the mist and spume of the waves against a grey and gloomy looking island rising into still greyer clouds. It was a long, monotonous and rough passage. Each cape we reached I thought would find Gizeram around the corner. Finally, we did turn in on the north side of one point to find a neatly layed out plantation and a number of European style houses. No one was about. It was Saturday afternoon and raining; raining hard.

Our colleagues were occupying one of the modern plantation houses and welcomed us warmly.[9] There is no question that such amenities as a refrigerator, hot water for a shower and running water from a tap provide some of the more basic pleasures of life.

It rained and blew hard throughout the weekend, which we spent in exchanging information and in sleeping. It was still blowing hard when I routed everybody out at 4.30 a.m. to embark on the Umboi, the larger of the two mission launches, which was to take several people round to Lab-Lab to catch the charter plane flown in from Lae every Monday. We were late in starting but the weather had ameliorated and the wind had died down quite a bit. Astern we towed a canoe to be dropped off with some Mandoks at their island.

After two hours we came into the shelter of Mandok Island and stopped to untie the canoe and allow the

Mandoks to go ashore. Joel and I had planned to disembark too but our late start meant that the passengers for the plane at Lab-Lab might miss it if too long a pause was taken to unload us, so we stayed on board. While the engine of the Umboi was loitering it suddenly died on us and our stern drifted on to the reef. The tide was ebbing. The luluai of the Mandoks, who was to disembark, with his men, grabbed the mast of a canoe lying along side and with several helpers used it to pole off our bows, which were ballooning us on to the reef. The canoe ran out an anchor to windward in the hope that we might winch off our stern. The engineer struggled with the filter of the engine's pump and eventually got the engine started again. We pulled away from the reef, but the engine was not running properly. The helmsman seemed to have difficulty in finding his passage through the reef. Sensibly, we turned back into the shelter of Mandok and anchored. It seemed clear that the party for Lab-Lab would miss their plane. Joel and I decided to go ashore, as originally planned. Later in the day the Karipo came down from Lab-Lab and took off the people destined for the plane. The Umboi returned to Gizeram. The plane did not fly to Lab-Lab that day, nor the next. In fact, the weather was so bad that the first plane from Lae didn't fly in until five days later: the mission at Lab-Lab was stuck with twelve visitors.

We stayed at the mission at Mandok Por (183) with the young Dutch priest and were joined by our colleague after he had seen his family safely to Lab-Lab.

The island of Mandok is larger than the two acres of Aramot, but not much larger. In 1963 there was a population of 343 living on an area less than four acres. The island is about a mile from the shore of the large island of Umboi on which the people have their gardens. Halfway between the shore and Mandok is a small island, less than two acres, on which the Catholic mission has built a small station and school. Each morning the children cross from Mandok to school and their canoes can be seen drawn up on the beach like a stack of bicycles.

On Mandok itself the houses are packed tight. There cannot be more than six feet between them, if that in some instances. A special section of the beach is reserved for the men with, behind it in part of the grove of palm trees which shelters the village from the southerly gales, a work house for the men where they sit and talk while making a net, spinning a line with the palm of the hand, rolling the thread on the knee, or carving a bowl. Some men seemed to do their carving under their houses, which are raised on piles some six feet from the ground. One house we found had one main corner post carved with a head comparable to the nausung masks we had seen in Kilenge (233, cf. 83) and certainly recalling earlier Tami work (87, 89, 234–236) and that of related cultures (90–94, cf. 95). The house post should be compared with Kilenge, (237–238, 241, 244–245) and Kombei versions (239–240; cf. 243). Whether under the house or in the men's area, there seemed to be a considerable amount of carving going on. One had the impression that Mandok was the main production centre of Siassi Island bowls, the bowls which formed such an important item of trade with New Britain (213–239). There were, I learned, some twenty-seven carvers

---

[9] Dr. and Mrs. Marshall Sahlins and Dr. Thomas Harding had been working for some time in the Siassi Islands and on the mainland. Their hospitality was greatly appreciated.

of whom at least six were recognized, in the Kilenge manner, as masters. The art of carving, they acknowledge, they learned from Tami, where carving is no longer pursued (201–204, 231–232).[10] In fact, it would seem that Mandok, and perhaps Aramot, largely fill the role today which was at one time performed by the Tami islanders (189–190, 192–200, 205–212, 223–231).

As well as bowls of different sizes, the Mandoks carve such objects as ladles, betel cups and spoons, combs, turtle shell armlets, bone knives, floats for nets, bailers (198, cf. 194–197), shields and the handles of adzes. They also make shell armlets. Quite elaborate decoration in low relief is given to some paddles (188), and canoe prows and sterns (183–187) as well as side-boards (191) are always finely carved. The islanders are a hardy, seafaring people and give great attention to the carving and finishing of their canoes (180–182).

During the first few days of our stay we experienced great difficulty in obtaining any specimens for a small collection of contemporary crafts we hoped to make for our museum. The people did not seem to like to sell anything with other people present. On a few occasions a man had paddled over to the mission by himself to negotiate a sale, usually in the early evening. Then, one afternoon, the Mandok reserve suddenly broke down completely. A large crowd gathered and thrust objects at us to buy. We had but a little money with us and soon ran out. A few people followed us across to the mission with more pieces still to sell. That night trading at the mission store was brisk. I noticed one carver bought a tin of mackerel, which seemed a strange item to trade to a people with such a rich harvest of fish to be had from the sea on their own door-step.

One day during our stay at Mandok, we rented the Umboi from the Lutheran mission to visit the island of Tuam, about an hour's run to the south. We took the precaution to assemble our primus and some rations and I took only one camera, in case we capsized. The weather looked bad. As we left the shelter of the reef the sea grew rougher and a massive black rain cloud swept rapidly up from the south towards us. When it closed with us the rain tore down and drove at us horizontally. The wind blew with a frightening fury so that the wallowing Umboi dipped her rails well into the boiling sea. Not knowing the capabilities of the tubby launch as a sea-boat, for she seemed ungainly, I wondered for some ten minutes whether we might not founder and be swept away to meet our maker. It hardly seemed possible that the storm could increase in force. Happily it was at its maximum and the Umboi creaked and groaned, and wallowed and shuddered on; and then rapidly the storm disappeared astern. It was typical of the sudden squalls that blow up so rapidly in this region; it left behind it a steady downpour of rain and a heavy sea pounding the windward side of the island of Tuam, the surf spraying the houses close to the beach. We anchored in the lee of Tuam, close to the shore, and not a

soul was to be seen. Tuam looked uninviting and a depressing place and when we did get ashore and walked round the village in the rain, our impressions remained. But rain puts a damper on any activity and nobody in his right mind, except an anthropologist, would ask people to show him their village in such miserable weather.

Tuam is much larger than Mandok and supports perhaps some five hundred people. While some carving is pursued it did not appear—at least in the course of our visit—that art was an activity pursued very strongly, as at Mandok (110, cf. 107–109).

It took us an hour and twenty-five minutes to reach Tuam but only fifty minutes to return with the sea astern. We were lucky, for as we came into the lee of Mandok and anchored, another black squall hit us, the rain just driving horizontally along the top of the sea.

After a week on Mandok and Mandok Por, we were due to fly back to Cape Gloucester from Lab-Lab. The Karipo was supposed to collect us the afternoon before to take us to Lab-Lab, but the day was nearly gone before she appeared from the north. We boarded her together with the lulai of Mandok and his son, Andrea, who had cut his arm badly the night before and whom we would leave on our way at Aramot, where there was a government medical orderly. As we began to close Aramot, the sky began to darken, prematurely, and a fresh squall of rain hit us. The mate wisely decided that we hadn't a hope of finding our way in through the narrow passage in the reef at Lab-Lab, so we anchored in the lee of Aramot to spend the night. Finding ourselves in the dark, with the rain beating against the canvas side screens and the launch full of copra sacks, left us somewhat depressed at the prospects of the night to come. Our camp beds were soaked from the rain, so we elected to stay on board, rather than struggle ashore to the haus kiap. The forecastle of the Karipo—which was really little more than a forepeak—had two bunks in it, but they were crawling with cockroaches. On the other hand, the waist and stern were full of copra sacks, all well soaked by driving rain from the storm. Cockroaches or copra beetles? We chose the latter and were proved right by subsequent experience with the former. But if you have ever slept on sacks of copra it is possible to debate the merits of aching bones versus knawed flesh.

Our good friend the luluai of Mandok, whom we had put ashore with his son, rustled up a kerosene lamp, without kerosene. Fortunately we had some, so were able to light our bizarre surroundings while we started up our portable primus to boil some water for soup and to heat a tin of beef steak and kidney pudding which we had with us. While we waited for the water to boil, and the rain beat down on us, the mate and his three sons, who ranged from eight to four years old, sat in the stern, eating cold taro. The programme from our transistor radio brought some odd emphasis to our strange situation. The mate and his sons withdrew to the forecastle and the cockroaches. We settled down with the copra bettles to enjoy a sample of the blessings of western man's insatiable demands for oil in one form or another, in this case, in its crudest, preliminary form. Sleep and wakening from aching bones, joints and muscles, gradually developed into a numbing confusion of somnolence and wakefulness, broken by an

---

[10] Since my visit in 1964, some Tami carvers have started working again, first at a village on the coast near Finschhafen and then some returned to the Tami Islands, I was told. The objects in illustrations 201–204 and 231–232 are examples of this new phase of Tami work, I was given to understand in Lae.

anxious quarter of an hour in the middle of the night when a squall hit us and the mate got up to let out more chain for the Karipo to ride the sudden blow.

At 4 a.m., the flesh really roused the spirit and demanded a total awareness of the real, physical world. The moon was shining and the Southern Cross stood clear in the heavens. At 4.45 a.m., I lit the primus and put on a kettle of water. The brew of coffee restored our circulation. By 5 a.m., it was beginning to get light. The mate began to check his diesel engine. We hailed the shore and, after a half an hour, a canoe put off to retrieve the lamp, which had lit our stormy vigil. Soon after 6 a.m. we up-anchored and sailed for Lab-Lab with a strong wind and swell astern. Thirty minutes later, before 7 a.m., we had the pleasure of wading ashore in pouring rain, for though a dinghy is kept at the buoy in the anchorage the method of its propulsion, as it has no rowlocks, is to send a small boy over the side to swim and push it; it is easier to wade, especially if it is raining.

The mission at Lab-Lab was hospitality itself . . . as it had been before. Fortified by a civilized breakfast of eggs and bacon and feeling optimistic, we waited for our plane from Lae. It suddenly came out of the clouds in a lull in the weather. Hoisting our cargo, everybody ran slipping through the mud for the airstrip, which the Lutheran missionary had gradually over the years cut out of the forest.

Very rapidly we were on board the Aztec with our cargo, away down the runway and over the sea. In a few minutes we were through the clouds and out into the welcoming sunshine over the Dampier Strait. Below were the white-capped waves of the rough sea, a sea with which we had battled but a week or so before. Ahead was New Britain. We felt a sense of returning home, heightened by the enjoyment of a brief flight, for, as we reached the coast, we flew over our five Kilenge villages and could see canoes on the shore and in the lagoon. It could not have taken more than twenty minutes before we circled in front of smoking Mount Langila and touched down on the barren air strip of Cape Gloucester. The Medical Assistant, to our surprise, met us with the Land Rover. A short step from the air strip, we found Nake and two men on the bush path: they had virtuously come to the beach with a canoe, as previously arranged, to pick us up. After the vagaries and vicissitudes of the Siassi Islands, we were much cheered to return to a land where everything, apparently, functioned. In the brief space of twenty minutes, we had crossed from an area currently enjoying its worst season of weather to one in which the annual cycle of seasons happened, at the time, to be most clement.

As we drove through the first village, the people waved and smiled at us, enhancing our sense of returning home. McSweeney's hospitality of lunch decided us to take a siesta before going about our work again. But the siesta was interrupted by the arrival of the young Patrol Officer, a lad of nineteen, tall, thin and agreeable but with a scruffy, rather meager beard. He had been on patrol the last two months, collecting the annual head tax. He organized his bed-sail on one side of the *haus kiap*, just under a hole in the roof which he did not notice, I suspect, and his policemen charged about 'our' spring-board floor, lashing the poles of his bed and shuffling his gear around in a military fashion. He dined with McSweeney and returned subsequently. But he had had a very bad boil in the groin for the last month of his patrol and decided to go in the Land Rover to Cape Gloucester and seek the Medical Assistant's care. We felt that his decision was sensible, for his boil was a nasty looking eruption; at the same time, his departure meant we would be on our own.

Change from Without

Although the Kilenge people are remote from the affairs of the modern world, for, happily, they are tucked away in a small corner, off the beaten track, nevertheless they are only still just off that track. They are very close to a dangerous corner and just round that corner is a roundabout as confusing as that around the Arc-de-Triomphe. Will man really conquer if he turns that corner?

Indeed; a piece of flotsam comes their way: they recognize that Alan Shepard exists, on a piece of paper, for there he is, whoever he is, and he is going to the moon. Perhaps not him, but some American will. And what are rockets which come from under the sea? Pora invented them. Perhaps the Kilenge made a mistake in driving out Pora to Australia. At least he didn't stay there although the Australians killed him. Now he is in America.

The Kilenge are on the edge of a new world. Up to now, they have been blessed by good fortune and have only had to make relatively minor adjustments. When the Japanese came, they took their families back into the bush, they said. Then the Americans came and drove out the Japanese. Here and there along the shore lie the rusting remains of some vessel. A Kilenge will tell you if it is Japanese or American. But the Americans soon went. Then Father McSweeney came and built up the Mission, its hospital and school; the church is a converted barrack left by the Americans. But the Kilenge were fortunate to be guided by the gentle hands of a humanist, who did not require them to make great changes in their ways and whom they could soon call the 'smiler'. The mission supply ship called once every three months and so did the Burns Philp trading vessel, the Paulus. A Kilenge crew soon learned to run the Leo, an old American work boat, for the good Father and the Kilenge captain of the Leo became the proud possessor of a coastal master's ticket. Sometimes the *balus*, the DC-3, would call at the Cape Gloucester airfield and the Kilenge became accustomed to mail coming to the mission whether by sea or plane. And sometimes a young priest, or Sister, would come on the plane and the Leo would sail along the coast to Bariai or Kaliai and leave him there at the mission. Father McSweeney would go on retreat once a year to Rabaul. Once, after he had been at Kilenge for ten years, he went away for quite a long time, for he went on leave. The easiest way to the outside world, the world of the Australians, was to go to the airfield and take the *balus*.

There were various ways to get to the airfield. It was a six mile walk along the beach and through the bush. If you borrowed McSweeney's bicycle you cut down the time by maybe a half hour, for there were six streams to ford and in many places the bicycle would sink into the soft, volcanic dust. Joel tried it; I didn't. The most pleasant and comfortable way to go was in the mission launch. The Leo would lie some two or three hundred yards off shore where there was a patch of deep water, clear of coral. She

[11] See Dark, 1969: 82–4.

could be reached by canoe or her dinghy but only when the south-east trades were blowing on the other side of the island. The dinghy was tied up astern. The captain stood on the forecastle, in the eyes, hanging on to the forestay, and with very slight hand orders to the helmsman in the wheel house conned the ship as he watched the channel through the coral.

One day, when we went in the Leo, she had to continue to Bariai so we took along a canoe in which to return. The canoe was a medium sized one from Siassi, for only the Siassi canoe's bow is fashioned so that it won't ship water when being towed, the Kilenge canoe being quite unsuitable (153). After a run of about twenty minutes at about nine or ten knots, the Leo anchored off the black sandy beach facing north at Cape Gloucester. We disembarked in the dinghy and set off through the bush. It is about a mile and a half to the strip with two streams to ford. The wait at the air strip can run into hours, depending on how late the plane is. The heat beats down and Langila, the volcano, smokes in small white puffs. Thoughts turn to the bottle of beer you can buy from the steward when the plane comes in but the Kilenge who came with us couldn't care less and are sound asleep. We made the return journey by canoe, poling close to the shore. Joel and I sat on the platform; one man poled in the bows, another in the stern and a third on the outrigger side of the platform. Our seamen, for all that much of their lives are spent on the water, seemed a bunch of land-lubbers. Our course zig-zagged all over the shallows. At one point our stern-man fell overboard; at another Joel's hat blew off; at still another we ran on to a coral outcropping which showed up quite clearly and could have been avoided. As we approached a patch where there was a bit of a swell with small waves, I clutched my camera and was all prepared to go over the side, after our performance up to that point. We waited for the waves and happily the right one was chosen and we were swamped. Few experiences can be more restful and pleasing to the senses than sailing along slowly in a canoe, looking down into the clear water and seeing the ever-changing formations of coral and fish: most striking is a small fish, of a brilliant cirulean blue, and the starfish: one also a brilliant blue, another like a cookie made for kids, cream colour with red 'icing' spots on it.

The Kilenge children, from about four years old up to sixteen, go to school at the mission where, under the native teachers, who are supervised by a nun, they are given elementary education in English. The curriculum is set by the Australian Administration and is standard throughout the Territory. The native teachers are recruited from different parts of New Guinea. At Kilenge, where was only one teacher who was a native of the place; two were Tolai and one was a Manus; the homes of the others I do not recall. A teacher can usually expect to be moved around every couple of years to a new school.

One day, at the Sister's request, we made a formal visit to the school, in school hours. She took us round each class room, of which there were eight, each one for a different age group. As we entered a classroom the pupils got up and said 'good morning, Sirs'. They were then made to say a poem or sing a song, which they did very well, but why teach them Killarney or a song about rabbits with all the accompanying actions, the nearest rabbit being two thousand miles away? The Sister, after all, was Irish.

After our visit to the classrooms a break was called. Some of the boys kicked a football around on a rough pitch. The *laplap*, or loincloth, is not suited to playing football: a small boy would be dribbling down the field nicely, get ready to shoot and his *laplap* would fall off; he would stop to recover it and lose the ball into the bargain. The girls didn't have quite the same problem, for they were playing rounders, or a version of baseball, which required only an occasional hitch, re-wrap or tuck-in of their *laplaps*.

A whistle was blown. The mid-morning break ended. The children all lined up in columns facing the flagstaff, largest in the front, smallest to the rear. We followed the Sister to the saluting point, sensibly placed under the shade of a tree. The columns picked up their dressing and stood at attention. 'God Save the Queen' was sung while the flag was hoisted, and followed with 'My Country'. They then marched off round the parade ground and into the class rooms, singing 'Mademoiselle from Armentiers, parlez vous' at the top of their voices: a flabbergasting innovation!

On Sundays the church at the mission was packed. The main service was at eight o'clock though a mass had been said earlier. The men sat on the left of the aisle, the older men at the back, the younger men in front, and in front of them the young boys. We sat with the elders on two benches at the back. On the right, a similar order pertains, though the married women with their very young children and those suckling infants form a solid rear half of the women's side of the church. A good half of the congregation were communicants. All the people were in their Sunday finery. Some of the men had put on a shirt. The young girls were in clean *laplaps* of brilliant scarlet or deep blue, worn round the hips, breasts bare and their hair freshly peroxided. One or two more prominent ladies of Kilenge society would put on a blouse for Sunday church. One Sunday morning, we saw Aisapo's daughter, who was late for church, hurrying along the beach, putting on a bra and being helped into her blouse, before strutting up to the mission in her finery. Half an hour after church she was stripped again to her *laplap*, her normal domestic attire.

After the mass, McSweeney delivered a sermon in Pidgin and hymns were sung. The choir consisted of all the young boys and girls in the front, with the congregation joining in strongly. The harmony of this massive congregation was excellent. One evening, shortly before our departure, we attended Vespers. The choir had been rehearsing specially so that we could record the service, which was a most moving experience: imagine yourself, brought up in the custom and habit of your local church, accustomed to psalms that resound and hymns, which— particularly at Christmas—bring emotions to common fulfilment; and then, suddenly, a new harmony, familiar,

appropriate, but somehow different, comes forth, expressing an already familiar emotion but in a new and satisfying form, fresh and vivifying, but intense, so that once felt it lives and echoes in the memory.

Prior to the arrival of the Patrol Officer on his annual inspection and collection of the head tax of ten shillings, there is a stir of activity in the villages while the people make copra to sell to the mission or cooperative store for the shillings they have to pay. All adult males have to pay the tax, though the chiefs and old men, we were given to understand, are exempted. In addition, there is generally some activity in house construction, for each house is supposed to have a separate cook house behind it. The *haus kiap* is supposed to be kept in repair. It is sufficient perhaps to show that 'Barkis is willing': the posts for a new *haus kiap* were put up when we were there and a large stack of timber for the flooring and sides of the house was left leaning against the posts but the structure was not taken beyond the foundations up to the time the Patrol Officer arrived.

On our last morning at Kilenge we were up at first light. From 7 a.m. to 9 a.m. Joel busied himself with Nake, taping some final work on Kilenge-Pidgin language equivalents. I wrote five pages of notes on what old man Tule had to say about many things. One felt that one was just at the beginning of learning something about the Kilenge and their culture and yet it was time to leave. To leave but to return, we hoped.

After many farewells on the beach, we boarded the Leo by dinghy and canoe. The Leo seemed full of people who had come to help us heft our cargo from the beach through the bush to the air strip and to bid us farewell. When we arrived at the lean-to on the edge of the strip, a fire was lighted and the Kilenge put the fish they had caught on the trip up in the Leo on its embers. Before it had been cooking for five minutes, the fish was removed and rapidly consumed. Our Kilenge friends curled up in the shade and went to sleep. The plane might come on time, but it might be one hour late, or two, or perhaps four, or not come at all. As the time approached noon our thirst mounted, for Nake had broken the thermos of water which the Sisters had kindly sent along. The Patrol Officer had come along to meet the plane and collect the mail. Conversation turned to the merits of different beers, a favourite subject with all Australians: unfortunately, neither of us were from Sydney or Melbourne so we were not in a position to maintain the merits of one city's brew over the other's.

The plane eventually came in, over two hours late. It was a solemn moment of going round shaking the hands of the eighteen Kilenge, and of old man Tule, their *luluai*, who had come to see us off.

Our return from Cape Cloucester in the DC-3 took us over the Siassi Islands, which sparkled below in the sun. Seeing them from several thousand feet up gave emphasis to their small size. The wash of a steamer altering course close to Tuam stood out as a white trail in the blue of the sea. Soon, we had landed at Finschhafen; and then, after a short pause, were off again to Lae, the end of the line directly connecting Australia and the world outside with New Guinea and the beginning of the line for those returning home.

Some Melanesian Pidgin Words

balus	a pigeon or airplane	*sospen*	a pot
haus kiap	an official guest house in each village	*tambu*	forbidden, taboo
laplap	a loincloth	*toktok*	talk, speech
luluai	the village chief, a government appointee	*tultul*	assistant village chief, a government appointee
meri	a woman or girl		
plet	a bowl, dish	*tumbuan*	a masked figure or mask
save	to know, to understand	*waitpus*	a paramount chief
singsing	a dance with singing		

References

BODROGI, TIBOR, 1961. **Art in North-east New Guinea.** Budapest: Publishing House of the Hungarian Academy of Sciences.

DARK, PHILIP J. C., 1969. The Changing World of the Kilenge, a New Guinea People. **Lore,** Vol. 19. No. 3: 74–89.
1970. South Sea Island Economics. **The Geographical Magazine,** Vol. XLII, No. 11: 787–794, August.

DARK, PHILIP J. C. and LORETTA R. HILL, 1966. Kilenge Paintings from Western New Britain *in* **New Guinea Paintings.** Southern Illinois University. (Catalogue to an Exhibition.)

The Dates of the Photographs

Photographs taken in 1964:

Nos. 4, 5, 9, 10, 17, 18, 33, 63, 67, 68, 70–74, 83, 106, 110–127, 131–137, 147–150, 154, 161, 162, 179, 183, 184, 187, 188, 191, 213–222, 233.

Photographs taken in 1966:

Nos. 3, 6–8, 15, 16, 19–21, 64, 69, 75, 99, 100, 144–146, 151, 157, 159, 160, 166, 169, 171, 175, 177, 194–197, 243–245.

Photographs taken in 1967:

Nos. 1, 11–14, 22–24, 26–32, 34–47, 54–62, 65, 66, 76–82, 84, 91, 101, 102, 138–141, 143, 152, 156, 158, 163–165, 167–168, 170, 172–174, 176, 180–182, 185, 192, 201–204, 223–224, 231, 232, 237–242.

Photographs taken in 1968:

Nos. 86, 87, 89, 92–98, 107–109, 189–190, 193, 198–200, 205–212, 229–230, 234–236.

Photographs taken in 1970:

Nos. 2, 25, 48–53, 85, 88, 103–105, 128–130, 153, 155, 225–228.

Notes to the Illustrations

1 *Village of Ulumaiinge with Mount Talawe behind*
Most Kilenge villages consist of two rows of houses separated by a 'street'. One row, where the village is coastal, as here, is close by the water's edge; the other would abut on the bush. Three of the houses have had palm fronds laid on their roofs, which are generally made of sago palm leaves obtained from Bariai, to give added protection during the inclement rainy season.

The forest covers Mount Talawe, which rises to 6,020 feet, all the way to the top from behind the village, providing the Kilenge with a variety of timbers for their different needs. There is a sufficient variety of woods to cater for special parts for a canoe or different beams for different parts of a house.

Mount Talawe is an extinct volcano, New Britain being very much an island of volcanoes, some of which are active. Close by Mount Talawe, on its eastern side, is Mount Langla (or Langila), which, every now and again, blows up, sometimes with a considerable fall out, but the Kilenge do not seem to take any notice when it does (see further in Dark, 1969).

2 *Approach to the village of Ongaia from the east*
The water in the foreground is where the sea meets a small stream across which is a bridge of logs providing entrance to the village from the east. In the distance can be seen Sakar Island. The Kilenge visit the two villages there from time to time.

3 *Entrance to Kilenge from the west*
The term Kilenge, while applying to the people themselves, their language and, in a general manner, to the five villages close together on the shore some six miles west of Cape Gloucester, also refers to two of them: the villages of Ulumaiinge and Waremo. The latter can be seen in the middle of the photograph, in the distance, beyond a line of light shining across the centre. In the foreground, to the right, can be seen a cross, which is in a graveyard. The Catholic mission has been active in the area since the 1930s and at Kilenge most of the people are baptized Christians.

4 *Kurvok and Portne villages at dawn*
The small house on piles in the water, in the foreground, is a latrine, an innovation of the Administration. To the right is a canoe, the new canoe of illustrations 149–150. Behind is another canoe and two small work boats belonging to the Catholic mission; the one on the right is the Leo.

5 *View of* HAUS PLIS, *copra shed and cooperative store*
The *haus plis*, which is on the right, is a rest house maintained by all villages for visiting policemen, who are usually those accompanying the patrol officer. The cooperative store is owned by the people who share its profits but its establishment and running is sponsored by the Administration.

The supplies to Kilenge come from Rabaul by a small tramp steamer of some 150 tons which is owned by the trading company, Burns Philp. The vessel trades along the south coast of New Britain to Kilenge, dropping off cargo and picking up copra. Trade items in the store varied in type and quantity: sometimes the store seemed well stocked with goods but more often than not it had but a few items, such as matches, tins of corned beef, rice, kerosene, an axe or two and some material for *laplaps*. The fortunes of the store tended to fluctuate depending on the energies of the local priest in stocking his store with competitive goods and his luck in maintaining his supplies from Rabaul by the mission supply ship.

The view is from the veranda of the *haus kiap* where the patrol officer and other official visitors stay when visiting the village. It is a structure very much like the *haus plis* though usually a little larger. At Kilenge these houses and the store with its copra shed were situated between the villages of Ongaia and Kurvok in a pleasantly shaded area called Malangon, just back forty yards or so from the shore.

6–8 *Woman making a handbag*
Men and women wear handbags for carrying their small personal possessions, such as a bit of tobacco and a piece of newspaper in which to roll it, a betel nut or pepper and a small tin with lime in it to go with the betel, perhaps a comb and a knife. The handbag, or *navesinga*, is made from part of the rib of the palm tree, the fronds being plaited, as in illustration 6. The corners are finished off, as in illustration 7, and then are tucked in. Illustration 8 actually pictures the stage reached before illustration 7, when the body of the *navesinga* has been finished but the loose ends have not been neatly braided. However, it shows the rib from which the plaiting was worked. This has to be split down the middle to provide the opening to the bag.

9–10 *Marakos of Ongaia making a basket*
Baskets are not usually made by the Kilenge of the coast but rather by those of the *lolo*, or the bush hinterland. Marakos, who was a master artist—he died in 1965—liked to turn his hand to them in his old age and made them beautifully. In illustration 9 he is shown sitting on the black volcanic sand under a house making *natika*, a basket, watched by some children too young to go to school. In illustration 10 he is shown just about to pull tight the weft element, which he has passed through the lower layer of warp, so that it secures the top one to it, the technique of making baskets being coiling.

11–14 *Basket-making in the Kilenge* LOLO
Illustration 11 shows a basket with the warp coiled loosely in the middle together with a few of the weft elements used to secure it. In bottom is the awl of the

basket-maker, who, in this case, was the *luluai* of Aragilpwa. The same basket, which is nearing completion is shown in illustration 12.

That in illustration 13 is 32.5 cms. in diameter and that in illustration 14 is 48 cms. The latter is close in size and design to the baskets pictured in illustrations 9–12.

15, 21 *House screens*

Two different designs of bamboo screens used as external walls of a house and internally, if there is any division into rooms. Compare with the screens in illustrations 17 and 18, or those in 5. The screens are of split bamboo, which are plaited, as is shown in illustrations 19–20.

16 *Building a new* HAUS KIAP *at Kilenge*

The task of building a new *haus kiap* rests in the hands of the *luluai* of a village, but, in this case, because Mr. Aisapo, the *waitpus*, the paramount chief of the Kilenge, lives in Ongaia village and he is a forceful administrator, he organized the construction of the house which is quite a job. The location in the bush of the different timbers needed has to be known; how many of each are required has to be worked out; parties of men have to be sent off to obtain them; who does what when and what materials are needed before others, all have to be considered before the work can get underway. But even prior to this, the design of the rooms, veranda, steps, the necessity to obtain good roofing materials from Bariai, have to be planned.

The illustration shows the main structure of the house has been erected and two screens, which form the rooms and walls of the house, are in position. (see *ills*. 15 and 19–21).

17 *Putting the finishing touches to a new house in Kurvok*

The two men on the roof are completing the covering of the ridge with a layer of sago thatch (cf. *ill*. 18). Kneeling on the ground is John Nasungewa who is sawing off the end of a floor beam (see next illustration). Steps will be placed to permit entry to the house at the position of his saw; behind is a veranda.

18 *Squaring off floor beams of a new house in Kurvok*

This shows the side of the house pictured in the previous illustration.

19–20 *Making a house screen*

Bamboos are cracked by hitting them sharply with a hammer and then split open to form the lengths which are plaited into a screen, as shown in illustration 19. The bamboo poles have all to be about the same size, in diameter, and, of course, cut to the same length in order to provide a uniform pattern. The material is somewhat recalcitrant and a hammer is useful to beat it into place much as a weaver of cloth will 'beat up' the weft with a sword or comb (*ill*. 20).

22 *Maleu of Kilenge with a headband of dog's teeth*

A headband such as Maleu has on is worn as part of a man's costume for the *singsing Sia* (see *ill*. 174). Up to the 1950s, it was common practice to pierce a person's ears. The resultant lobe would be cut and small rings of turtle shell be put on each length of lobe, the two then being stuck together so that they would heal back again as one (cf. *ill*. 23). The chain around Maleu's neck was bought at the mission store and would have some Catholic emblem on it.

23 *Donga of Ulumaiinge with her grandchild*

Donga is the wife of Talania of Ulumaiinge, the big man of his village. She is a much respected person. Here she is pictured costumed for the *singsing Sia* and holding her son's child in a pause in the proceedings. The necklaces she is wearing are lengths of shell money. One is of a dark brown shell, the other of a white one. A length requires hundreds of small shells. The shell money is made by the Kombei and obtained through trade (see Dark, 1970). It used to be a vital item in the brideprice, at least five fathoms being required.

Around her left biceps Donga wears a bead armband imported from Hong Kong (probably). Tucked into it, as into an armband on her right arm, are leaves of plants put there for decorative purposes.

24 *Aisapo of Ongaia*

Mr. Aisapo, who was the *waitpus*, the paramount chief of the Kilenge, and who is a Councillor for Kilenge now that the system of local government has been introduced into the area, is shown here adzing the blade of a paddle. He is recognized as a *namos tame*, a master artist, and is skilled at all the tasks an artist turns his hands to, but particularly in architecture and nautical matters, producing the finest of houses and canoes.

25 *Makele of Ongaia*

Makele was the second eldest of Marakos' three sons. Like his father was, he is a master artist. He carved the masks pictured in illustrations 85, 88 and the bowl in illustrations 225–228.

26–27 *Mundua of Portne*

The cicatrization marks on Mundua's face are made with a razor blade, charcoal being rubbed into the cuts. Formerly, obsidian, which was traded from Talasea, was used to make the cuts. Her hair is bleached with a peroxide bought from the local store, or, failing that source of supply, the juice of a lemon was used. The two necklaces are imported, probably originating from Hong Kong. Mundua is the wife of Nagalo of Portne.

28–29 *Akisa of Portne*

Akisa is the wife of Serek of Portne. The choice of cicatrization marks is a personal one and girls tend to follow a fashion, one design being copied among friends. Akisa's necklaces are of imported beads.

30 *Luguvia of Portne costuming for a* SINGSING

As well as their faces women decorate their bodies and

legs with cicatrization marks. Luguvia has gone a bit further than most in the extent of the markings on the medial side of her breasts. Her hair is a shade of red. On her right arm she wears a bracelet of imported beads and below it one made of a particular vine found in the bush and usually traded from the Siassis. She is shown with only part of the full costume she will put on for the *singsing* (cf. *ill.* 60).

31 *Mundua of Ongaia*

Mundua is the daughter of Talania and Moyo of Ongaia. In addition to the traditional designs on her chest she has marked names of friends on her arms both by cicatrization and burns with the end of a cigarette. Her necklace has opposum teeth threaded with imported beads.

32 *Cicatrized back*

33 *Making a shell bracelet*

The picture illustrates a woman sitting under a house in Ongaia engaged in the first stages of making shell bracelets. Trochus shells, collected from the reef, are used. The cone has to be removed and then the centre. This is done by using a stone and percussion. When the shell is reduced to a flat surface, as is shown in the illustration, embers from a fire are placed in the centre to soften the shell and make it easier to knock out with a stone.

34 *Giarop of Portne*

She has stuck in her hair the end of a cigarette, made by rolling tobacco in newspaper.

35 *Tiele of Portne*

It is not easy to estimate old people's age but Tiele appeared to be just about the oldest woman around and needed a stick to walk with.

36 *Cicatrized back*

37–39 *Making shell bracelets*

Illustration 37 shows a woman—a visitor from Mandok staying in Kurvok—grinding down the side of the shell ring on a gray stone using the gray volcanic grit around her as an abrasive with water.

When the grinding and smoothing process has been completed, the edge of a bracelet is incised with linear designs by means of a knife. Black is rubbed into them to enhance them against the white shell background (cf. *ills.* 216–217).

40–47 *Kilenge and Mandok turtle shell armlets*

Sizes, 43–44, ht., left, 12.3 cms., rt. 11 cms; 44–45, ht.

While the Kilenge will use the plates of any turtle caught locally, they also obtain them from the Kombei to the east and the Siassis to the west as an item of trade. The plates are carved and then bent into the form of an armlet. The bending is done by immersing the shell in hot water and tying it around a cylindrical piece of wood of the same size as an ordinary arm. When the turtle shell finally reaches the required form of an armlet, lime is rubbed into the low relief designs and wiped off, leaving them to stand out.

The left hand armlet of illustrations 40–43 is of particular interest as it shows the markings of a *nausung* mask, in fact, that of Talania of Kurvok. Such markings and the mask form of which they are a part should be compared with similar representations from Tami to the west of Kilenge, for example (cf. *ills.* 87, 89, 96–98 and 233–238, 241), and as represented on the side of a men's house in the Vitu Islands to the east (cf. *ill.* 243), in fact, the easternmost extremes of the distribution of this motif, representing, in a generalized context, two culture heroes, Mooro and Aisipel, as the Kilenge refer to them. The former had the head of the man and the body of a snake; the latter was like an ordinary man (cf. *ills.* 239–240).

The mask form is not easily recognizable in the right hand armlet of illustrations 40–43 but is there, in an abstract form; the snake is more readily apparent. This armlet was carved in Mandok, in the Siassis, the others in Kilenge.

In illustrations 44–47, on the left hand armlet, the artist has absorbed the Christian symbol of a cross into a traditional design. The general design does not relate to the mask form and snake represented in the two armlets in illustrations 40–43, but the mask form and the snake occur in the right hand armlet of illustrations 44–47, even though not clearly apparent in the illustration; they are 'hidden' by the complexity of the design which embraces two other other major motifs, the crocodile and a bird. The latter, in janus form, a feature of the art of the area, is apparent at the top of the armlet.

48–53 *Kilenge turtle shell armlets*

Sizes, left, ht. 8.3 cms; middle, 6.8 cms; rt. 12 cms.

The mask form referred to in illustrations 40–47, is obscure in the armlet on the left, non-existent in that in the centre and somewhat abstract in that on the right, but in all three the snake motif is represented. The crocodile form of the armlet on the right in illustrations 44–47 occurs in a more abstract manner in the armlet on the left in illustrations 48–53 (see *ill.* 47). On the centre armlet pig's tusks are clearly carved (cf. *ill.* 165).

54 *Kilenge turtle shell armlets*

Sizes, left, top, ht. 5.2 cms; bottom, 7.2 cms; rt., top, 7 cms; bottom, 4.8 cms.

While the mask form and snake, referred to in illustrations 40–43, occur on the two armlets pictured on the left, only the snake is represented in the two on the right.

55 *Kilenge turtle shell arm-rings*

Ht. 5.6 cms.

The rings are made into the form of a bracelet by being braided together with a plant fibre.

56 *Kilenge armbands*

Width, across braided portion, 12 cms.

These are plaited from a black plant fibre said to occur in the Siassis (on Umboi Island) from whence they are obtained in trade.

57–58 *Preparing a dance skirt*
The leaves of a plant, which have been sun-dried, are teased out and the stems split, as shown here. The woman working is from Ongaia, a daughter of *luluai* Tule.

A Mandok woman, a visitor to Kurvok, is shown rubbing the dye of a yellow root, which she has crushed on the stone in her basket, into teased-out fibres. The Kilenge say they prefer to boil the material and dye in a pot.

59 *Preparing a dance skirt*
Another Mandok visitor shown stitching parts of a dance skirt together.

60 *Donga of Ulumaiinge in dance skirt*
Donga, wife of Talania of Ulumaiinge, is all dressed up for a *singsing*. As well as the tutu shown being made in illustrations 57–59, she wears turtle shell arm rings, a shell one and an imported bead one, and various plant fibres (cf. *ill.* 23).

In the background are pieces of second world war air-stripping which were laid down by the Americans on the Cape Gloucester air-strip. Here they are shown used as a fence to a Christian graveyard located just to the west of Ulumaiinge (cf. *ill.* 3).

61 *Woman of Kurvok in dance skirt*
The woman in the foreground is costumed similarly to Donga in the previous illustration except that her plaited armlet is of indigenous manufacture. Round her buttock is a cord made of plant fibres used to secure her skirt.

62 *The village of Ongaia*
This picture of the village of Ongaia was taken from the air. It shows the passage through the reef, which shelters Kilenge to seaward. Much of the bush, in the foreground, has been cleared and planted with palm trees for cropping coconuts, the only cash crop of the Kilenge. But it is only areas close to the shore which have been so planted, the bush further back up the mountain being used for gardening.

63 *Clearing the bush for a garden*
Clearing the bush for a garden is very heavy work as is evidenced by the photograph. Trees have to be cut down and branches, brush and small logs burned off: a fire is burning in the background on the right of the photo. The size of the tree in the centre is very apparent when compared with those of the two men standing close by it. The poles on the left are the remains of a platform which was erected for cutting down the tree.

64 NATAPTAVO *mask*
This mask, which is called *sukovilim*, is said to have come from Kaliai (see Dark & Hill, 1966). It is shown here pausing at Malangon, the place where the *haus kiap* is located, in the course of its tour of Ongaia, Kurvok and Portne to promulgate the *waitpus' tambu* on picking coconuts. The mask is kept in Portne. It is made of coconut bast stretched on a frame, the design being painted on the bast. The wearer can see just a little bit through the holes in the bast fibre. The mask fits over the head on to the shoulders over which the cloak of banana leaves is placed.

65 NATAPTAVO *masks dancing at a* SINGSING
These two masks belong to Kilenge, that is, to the two villages of Ulumaiinge and Waremo where they perform a function similar to that of *sukovilim* in Ongaia, Kurvok and Portne (see *ill.* 64). They are both called *wagili* and are said to have come from Talasea. In this photograph they are shown performing at a *singsing* at Malangon. They dance with arms linked through their leaf cloaks. In their free hand each holds a plant stalk with the leaves tied. The decorative 'crests' to the masks are made of the feathers of the cockatoo, chicken and bird of paradise, feathers of the last being a rare decorative device for the bird does not exist on New Britain so that the plumes had to be traded in from mainland New Guinea.

66 WAGILI *masquerader resting*
The cloak is heavy and the mask hot, necessitating a rest from time to time. The masquerader's spear is stuck upright in the sand.

67 NATAPTAVO *mask and cloak*
This mask, which is called *aigilo*, has just been taken out of the men's house, the entrance to which is on the left, and has been put on top of the masquerader's cloak preparatory to being put on. The mask is shown being worn in illustration 68. It is made in a similar manner to that in illustration 64.

68 NATAPTAVO *masqueraders in Portne*
On the left are two masks called *mundip;* the third from the left is the mask pictured in the previous illustration; on the right is *sukovilim* but a 1964 version of the mask, not the one shown in illustration 64, which was in use two years later, for the mask had been re-painted. *Sukovilim* carries a spear of bamboo. The masks are dancing close by the two men's houses in Portne. The white crests of the masks are of chicken feathers. Below, on *mundip*, are cassowary feathers, and on *aigilo*, feathers stuck into a 'topknot' of vegetable fibres; below this is a ring of dog's teeth.

69 NATAPTAVO *masqueraders at Cape Gloucester*
The masks shown here are similar to those pictured in the previous illustration but are from a different place. They performed at the Cape Gloucester patrol post on the occasion of the opening of a small hospital which is normally staffed by a Medical Assistant and first aid and nursing orderlies.

70–72 *Masqueraders costuming at Birik, Umboi Island*

Illustration 70 shows the very long shoulder cloak of shredded pandanus leaves which the masquerader is about to put on. In the background is the men's house where the masks are kept. The sides of the houses, as elsewhere on Umboi and the Siassis, are of planks (cf. *ill.* 242). Illustration 71 shows finishing touches being put to the costumes of the three masked figures. Illustration 72 shows one of the masks, which can be compared with the Kilenge version of the same theme (cf. *ill.* 68). I do not know whether this form of conical mask occurred on mainland New Guinea or not, but if it did, or does, it may well have derived from New Britain as did these masks on Umboi Island. Closely similar are the more rounded *tago* masks, which used to exist on the Tami Islands, sometimes in a janus form, and which were said to have been obtained from West New Britain (see *ills.* 96–98). There is no evidence for a janus form of the *nataptavo* mask having been made by the Kilenge though janus themes do appear in Kilenge art.

73 SINGSING *begins at Birik, Umboi Island*

After costuming by the men's house, the masqueraders were led off to the village centre, or 'square', accompanied by the chorus of men playing their drums.

74 *Mask on Tamuniai Island*

This mask was made of a number of bamboo slats, made by splitting bamboo rods down the middle. These were held together by wrapping them horizontally with thread made of a vegetable fibre. The design, which designates the mask as *aikoskiwe*, is painted on. The mask is worn in a fashion similar to other *nataptavo* masks of the Kilenge, with a shoulder cloak.

75 *Masquerader at Cape Gloucester*

In August 1966, there was a *singsing*, which was sponsored by the patrol officer, at Cape Gloucester. The mask pictured here appeared. I thought it was a Kombei mask, as the people of Tamuniai did not divulge the origin of their mask in 1964 (*ill.* 74). This mask was acknowledged as from the Kilenge *lolo* and the Tamuniai mask as having been bought by the Kombei from the Kilenge *lolo* just as the *nataptavo* masks, which they also had, had been bought from Kilenge.

76–77 NAUSUNG *dancing at Malangon, Kilenge*

The mask, called Mooro, was made by Nake of Portne under the guidance of Talania of Ongaia (see *ills.* 78–81) and is similar to his mask (cf. *ill.* 82). The crest is of chicken feathers and the black 'tuft' below is of cassowary feathers. In the days before European contact the dancer was bare to the waist but since German times he has worn a shirt which is stuffed to make the dancer look fat. The Kilenge also like the masquerader to wear trousers which are too big for the dancer so that these too can be padded and make *nausung* look fat and well fed.

78–81 *Talania of Ongaia, master artist, carving a* NAUSUNG *mask*

Talania of Ongaia, *namos tame*, master artist, is pictured working on a *nausung* mask, which is shown painted in illustration 82. In illustration 78 he is shown using a knife.

82 *Painted* NAUSUNG *mask*

The mask is shown painted but without the feathered crest which is put on when the mask is danced, as in illustrations 76–77. It is the painted designs which distinguish one *nausung* mask from another: notably the marks around the eyes and the forehead marks. Mask designs belong to families. This mask is called *marimbu aiinge* which Talania got from his mother's family.

83 NAUSUNG *masks*

These two painted wooden masks belong in the family of the late Mr. Pano, who was the traditional big man of Portne, the oldest of the five Kilenge villages. They were carved before the second world war and are two of only four such masks to survive the Japanese occupation. The one on the right is called *senkana* and the one on the left, *sago* or *agamaiya*.

84 *Four* NAUSUNG *masks in Waremo*

These four masks were being carved under the sponsorship of Navona, the traditional big man of Waremo.

85, 88 NAUSUNG *masks, Ongaia*

These masks were carved by Makele of Ongaia, *namos tame*, in November and December, 1970. They were decorated by Makele's younger brother, Ailama, with crests of plumes similar to that on the mask in illustrations 76–77. The small one is called *nausung umbum;* the other is *nausung aisiwok*. The backs of these two with a third called *nausung kaiwoka*, are shown in illustration 88. The height of the small one, to the crown of the head, is 41 cms.

86 *Wooden masks (Wuppertal)*

The painted wooden masks on the left and right, which were collected by missionaries, are assumed to be from the Tami islands on the basis of their similarity to known masks from Tami, such as noted in the Rautenstrauch Joest Museum, Köln, or when compared with figures 26, 27 and 30 in Tibor Bodrogi's *Art in Northeast New Guinea*, Budapest, 1961. That in the centre, on the other hand, probably derives from Astrolabe Bay.

If these three masks are compared with the Kilenge *nausung* masks and those in the illustrations which follow (87 and 89–98), although there is quite some variation to be noted among them, there are formal relations sufficient to warrant considering all these masks as of a related style. The Tami masks ceased to be made soon after contact and initial missionary activity—on either side of the 1900s. Those of the Astrolabe Bay region which survive to us probably all derive from those early days but the trait persisted in regions culturally related but outside missionary influence, or resistant to it. It would seem that the missionaries happened to be most active at the centre, or centres, from whence the trait originated, or was most actively developed, namely Tami and, perhaps, Astrolabe Bay. Indeed, the latter may well have been the initial focus.

Reference to the map will show that the trait covered a pretty extensive geographical area—Astrolabe Bay—Umboi Island—Tami Islands—West New Britain and the Vitu Islands—if consideration is given to illustrations 87–98, which follow, as well as those that went before (*ills*. 76–85).

87   *Wooden mask* (*Mission Museum, Wuppertal*)

This wooden mask is also shown in illustration 86, centre. To be noted is the exaggeration given to the ears, which were pierced in real life so that the lobe often hung down quite a bit (e.g. *ill*. 28). Representation of this feature varies and is formalized a bit differently in different places. The eyes of this mask are 'opened' below the actual eye socket.

89   *Tami-style mask*

This mask, 57 cms. in height, was carved by Makele of Ongaia, *namos tame*, and shows a close similarity to the Field Museum mask in the next illustration (90). It is in fact a copy of that mask, the Kilenge version of it, as seen from a post card, which I sent to Kilenge in 1967. Months later the mask appeared in the mail as a gift from Makele and Ailama of Ongaia, having been sent by parcel post. The eyes were not cut through as they are in the Field Museum piece and Makele has, in fact, changed certain forms quite a bit, if close comparison between the two masks is made. Particularly to be noted is the 'top-knot', to which the plumes of *nausung* are attached, and the protruding tongue, both of which features are essential to Kilenge *nausung* masks. The painting of the two, in red, black and white, is similar.

90   *Tami-style mask* (*Field Museum of National History*)

This mask, which is 61 cms. in height, is variously designated as from the Huon Gulf or Tami Islands. Whether collected in the Tami Islands by A. B. Lewis before the first world war or by the missionary, Balmer, on Umboi Island is not certain. Lewis, following information given by Balmer, noted that this mask was 'used by the natives of Rook Island' (another name for Umboi Island) 'and corresponds to the *tago* masks of Tami' (see *ills*. 96–97). 'The Tami Islanders sometimes make them as ornaments on the roof of the special *lum* erected at the time of the *balum* or circumcision cere-monies' (exhibition notice, Field Museum). *Lum* is the word for a men's house; the Kilenge term is *naulum*. The Lutheran missionaries were early in to Umboi Island, first contact being from about 1898, but they never crossed the Dampier Strait to West New Britain, to missionize.

91   *Mask from Umboi Island* (*Basel*)

This carved and painted mask is known through its appearance in one or two publications. It was collected in the period between the two world wars and is an important piece, being documented as from Umboi Island. There are however one or two other masks closely similar to it in style which were collected by American Lutheran missionaries. Together with that in illustration 94 they provide examples of the variations of the style range of the general area. The ear form of this mask is intermediary between that of Astrolabe Bay and the Kilenge (cf. *ills*. 87–88). It has the spike on top of the head which is found on Kilenge masks but which is absent from some Astrolabe Bay and Tami ones (cf. 87 and 90).

92–93   *Kilenge* (?) *mask* (*Cologne*)

This wooden mask is noted in the catalogue of the Rautenstrauch-Joest Museum (Nr. 48160) as from West New Britain and was probably made before the first world war. It was in the collection of the Museum für Völkerkunde, Berlin, before going to Cologne, being illustrated in Eckart von Sydow's *Die Kunst der Naturvölker und der Vorzeit*, published in Berlin in 1923. It seems highly likely that it is an early Kilenge piece, for it has the tongue sticking out, which seems to be a Kilenge trait and is certainly a characteristic of known Kilenge *nausung* masks. In addition, it has markedly protruding 'spikes' to the ears, a feature which varies on Tami-style masks but is more prominent on Kilenge ones though never as highly placed as on this one. The spike protruding from the top of the head is a feature of Kilenge masks though it was noted for the Basel specimen in the previous illustration, the mask from Umboi, and occurs on Astrolabe Bay ones as well (see *ills*. 87 and 91). The mask is 60 cms. in height, not counting the spike on the top, and 30 cms. wide.

94   *Rai Coast mask* (*Cologne*)

This painted wooden mask is noted in the Rauten-strauch-Joest Museum catalogue (Nr. 37802) as coming from the village of Kiari on the Rai coast. It is 54 cms. high. Its mouth and nose seem closely comparable to the Basel specimen (cf. *ill*. 91). It can be compared with Kilenge(?) mask in illustration 92 as the two were exhibited side by side in Cologne. That the mask was collected on the Rai coast does not necessarily mean that it was carved there. It could have been carved in the same place or area as the Basel specimen, which, equally, might not have been carved on Umboi Island even if collected there, for masks were traded. It does seem likely that the mask of illustration 92 was carved in West New Britain for it is comparable to masks known to be carved by the Kilenge.

95   *Mask from the Vitu Islands* (*Cologne*)

This carved and painted mask, which is 58 cms. high, is noted in the Rautenstrach-Joest Museum's catalogue (Nr. 20767) as coming from West New Britain and probably the French Islands, which are also called the Vitu Islands. The mask is typical of the Vitu style: I have seen one in a men's house on Garove Island, in 1966, which was a close representation of the type (see *ill*. 159). There are one or two examples in museum collections. The type seems to represent one extreme of the style range of masks for the general area. In the Field Museum there is a version of the same kind of mask but constructed on a frame, covered with coconut bast and painted, a form similar to the Kilenge *natautavo* type or the Tami *tago* ones.

96–97 *Tami* TAGO *mask (Wuppertal)*

The Tami *tago* masks belonged to families, each having its own design, just as with the Kilenge and their *nausung* masks. The similarities of the marks around the eyes on masks from both places are notable (cf. *ill.* 82). In fact, A. B. Lewis noted before the first world war that masks were said to have been acquired by the Tami islanders from West New Britain, through marriage. The Kilenge generally acknowledge that their *nausung* masks came from the Siassis (see *ills.* 70–72), or Tami, including Umboi Islands in the Siassis. As at Kilenge with *nausung*, women and children on Tami were forbidden to see the *tago* masqueraders on pain of death. Lewis noted sixty years ago that the meaning of the *tago* masks was not clear. This one, like a number of others, has a nose of carved and painted wood which is attached to the face. On the nose is a snake.

98 *Tami* TAGO *masks (Neuendettelsau)*

Two examples of *tago* masks from the Tami Islands are pictured with long shoulder cloaks worn in a fashion similar to that noted for the Kilenge *nataptavo* masks but in contrast to the costume of the *nausung* masqueraders, who only wore a 'skirt' of leaves (cf. *ills.* 76–77). The top of the *tago* masks is similar to that of Kilenge *nataptavo* ones, including a crest of cassowary feathers, as shown here, and, usually, also the plume of white feathers which is not shown.

99 *Talania of Ongaia adzing a drum*

The artist of this drum was really Nake of Portne. Here Talania is giving him a hand partly because he is a friend of Nake's and partly because artists help each other out. While Nake may not be a *namos tame* as is Talania, Nake is skilled at carving hour glass drums, having produced many in the past.

100 *Finished carving of a drum*

This illustration and the next show the drum which Nake completed, lime having been rubbed into the low relief designs to enhance their decorative effect, black having been put on the marks under the eyes and the head of the drum, which is the skin of a lizard, having been stuck on. The faces on the drum, with the snakes reaching to each chin, indicate that a *nausung* character is meant to be represented. In this case it is Mooro, which is the name of the Kilenge culture hero—referred to in the notes to illustrations 40–47. The story of him and his brother Aisipel occurs in one form or another throughout the area from Madang to Talasea (cf. *ills.* 239–240).

101 *Three Kilenge drums*

The drum on the left is that pictured in illustrations 99–100. It is 79 cms. high. The drum in the middle, which is minus the head, belongs to Aisapo. It has only the one mask carved on it. The drum on the right, which belonged to Kaiwoka and now belongs to Talania of Kurvok, is a superb piece of carving. The two heads, by the handle, represent Kaiwoka's *nausung* (see next illustration). The drum on the left was carved of a wood of the Borage family; the other two were made from a *Calophyllum*.

102 *Detail of 'Kaiwoka's' drum*

The snake motif noted on the drum in illustration 100 can be seen in the narrow angle, or peak, of the design pointing upward, above two eye forms.

103–105 *Drum*

This drum, which is slender and light in weight, belongs to Makele of Ongaia, who carved it.

106 SINGSING *to* BUKUMO *in Kurvok*

The old men are singing to *bukumo* which is now ready to be danced in Portne.

107–109 *Two Tami drums (Neuendettelsau)*

These two drums from the Tami Islands should be compared with the Kilenge drums pictured in the previous illustrations as well as with illustration 110. The theme of the two brothers is clearly symbolized in the larger of the two drums which is remarkably similar to that illustrated next (110) which I saw on the island of Tuam in 1964. When the Tami drum was collected and sent to the mission museum at Neuendettelsau is not known.

110 *Siassi drum*

This drum was seen in 1964 on the island of Tuam, the largest of the Siassi Islands.

111 BUKUMO *being constructed in Portne*

This is the other side of the janus mask, *bukumo*, from the one shown in illustration 113. The face of the mask is coconut bast, which is painted white, and the design of the face is painted on in red and black colours. The nose is a carved janus lizard.

112 BUKUMO *dancing in Portne*

Bukumo is shown in the street connecting Kurvok and Portne villages on his way to dance in the 'square' at Portne where the drummers have assembled, as shown in this illustration. The masquerader's left arm can be seen protruding from the cloak of leaves. It is steadying one of the two poles which come down on either side of his body and enable him to control the mask. The frame to which the poles are attached rests on his head and is heavy. The masquerader walks or hops in an up and down motion which causes the giant feather fan to sway fore and aft in a closing and opening motion.

In the photograph can be seen quite a few children gathered at the feet of the drummers. The children were fascinated, never having seen the mask before.

Bukumo is indigenous to the Kilenge but the people of Umboi Island used to make the mask before the first world war.

113 BUKUMO *being constructed in Portne*

One of the artists, who worked on constructing *bukumo*, is sitting on the other side of the mask, putting a finishing touch to the shredded pandanus cape which hangs down to cover the upper half of the masquerader: the artist's right leg can be seen on the ground. The frame of the mask, which is here propped up under the cape, and the canes with the feathers are the component parts of the mask which are kept wrapped up in the men's house.

41

The rest of the mask is constructed afresh each time that it appears. The feathers are those of the fishing eagle, *saumoy* and the toucan.

114–115 *Nake of Portne drawing mask designs*
Nake is shown here on the veranda of the *haus kiap* drawing out two mask designs with marking inks. The completed designs are shown in the next illustration.

The design on the left is for a *nausung* mask, *moyel*, which is no longer made. On the right is Nake's version of the *nataptavo* mask, *sukovilim* (cf. *ill.* 64). Behind his right shoulder are the steps to the veranda of the *haus kiap*.

116 *Canoe designs*
These two designs, which Nake drew, are for the prow or stern of a canoe. The one on the left, which is pictured in illustrations 140–141, is called a crab; the one on the right is a fish's tail.

117, 122 *Canoe designs*
Further canoe designs drawn by Nake. The one on the left is called by the name of an insect; the one on the right represents the tail of a garfish.

118 NAUSUNG *design*
This design was drawn by Talania of Ongaia and represents a *nausung* called *kaikai*, which, though a Melanesian Pidgin term meaning food, is used by the Kilenge. The marks below the lower lip are said to represent human blood, for *nausung kaikai* eats human flesh (see Dark & Hill, 1966).

119 NAUSUNG *design*
This design was drawn by Talania of Ongaia and represents a *nausung* called *kanamure*, which forms a pair with *kaikai*, the *nausung* of illustration 118. *Kanamure* is owned by Aisapo.

120 NAUSUNG *design*
This was drawn by Talania of Ongaia. It represents *nausung aisiwok*. As with *kaikai* (*ill.* 118), the marks from the lower lip are said to represent the blood of men who have been killed and eaten by *aisiwok*.

121 NATAPTAVO *mask designs*
These are drawn by Talania of Ongaia. Both masks are called *nagiltung* and were created by Talania and Baule. The one on the right is pictured with a dance club which would be similar to those shown in illustrations 128–130.

123–126 NATAPTAVO *mask designs*
This was drawn by the late Mr. Pano and represents *vuvil* (123).

These were drawn by Aisapo. The one on the left he called *aisipel* and the one on the right *vure* (124).

Drawn by Nake. Both, he said, were called *aigilo*. (125).

Drawn by Nake. They are both referred to as *wagili* and are said to have come from Talasea. The two masks are shown dancing in illustration 65 (126).

127 NATAPTAVO *mask designs*
Drawn by Nake. Both are called *tambu* and are said to originate from Talasea (*ibid*).

128–130 *Kilenge dance club*
These dance clubs were carried by masqueraders, as shown in illustration 121. The longest of them is 98 cms. *Nausung* designs decorate the tops of the clubs (*ill.* 129) and the snake of the Mooro theme is present on each.

131 *Two canoes in Ongaia*
The larger of the two is a sea-going canoe, which belonged to Marombe and was painted by the late Marakos, *namos tame* of Ongaia. He is pictured making a basket in illustration 10. The smaller is for inshore work and fishing on the reef.

132 *Stern of large canoe of illustration* 131
The main motif is called *kamor*, which is also a man's name and the name of an insect (cf. *ills.* 117, 122).

133–134 *Bow of large canoe*
The scroll motif is said to represent any line or rope. The pattern between this and the name represents the cane of which the leaf is used to make the material for a woman's dance skirt (cf. *ill.* 57).

135 *Stern of Bariai canoe*
The canoe belongs to a big man from Baria who is visiting Aisapo on his return from a trip to Sag-sag. It is pictured in the distance in the next illustration.

136–137 *Stern of large canoe*
This canoe belonged to *luluai* Tule of Ongaia. It was made and painted under *namos tame* Marakos' direction. The main motif is referred to as *raiila* and represents the underwing of a pigeon. The squiggly design of the close-up photo of illustration 137 represents a fern found in the bush.

138–141 *Small canoe*
The illustrations show bow and stern of a small canoe seen at Cape Gloucester but with no owner around to ask about the designs, which seem to be typically Kilenge. The crab design, in illustrations 140–141, was referred to under illustration 116.

142 *Adzing hull of new canoe*
This canoe was to be a sea-going one. It was about 14 metres long and the adzing of the hull was heavy work but many of the middle-aged men of Portne, who were skilled with axe and adze, gave a hand. The iron adze blade shown being used was one dating from the days of the Germans and considered highly by the Kilenge, who complained at them no longer being available. The canoe, and the workers, are sheltered from the heat of the noon

day sun, which would be directly overhead, by a lean-to which can also be seen in the next illustration. The shelter shades the wood and prevents it from drying out too quickly. The canoe is being made by Mesel, who was *luluai* of Portne.

143, 152   *Painting a canoe*
Anavoga of Waremo is shown painting a new canoe. The completed motif in the panel is called 'top of the mountain'. The paints he is using are red, black and white and are indigenous. His palette is half a coconut shell and his brush the stem of a plant of which the fibres have been chewed to soften them.

144   *New canoe*
The illustration shows the prow of Mesel's new canoe in Portne. The principal motif represents *nasok*, a garfish (cf. *ill.* 122). The colours are red and blue on a white ground and were painted by Nake and Pano of Portne.

145   *Painting a canoe*
Aigilo of Ongaia is shown holding two coconut palettes in his hands and pausing from painting his new canoe. The design of the main panels is the same as was noted in illustration 132; it is interspersed with the same motif which was put on the canoe in the previous two illustrations.

146   *Renewing the lashings*
The large boom poles which are lashed to the hull and go out to provide the main support of the outrigger are here seen having their lashings refurbished. The canoe is Mesel's.

147–148   *Renewing lashings of canoe outrigger support*
New lashings and a new support for the outrigger are seen being attached by a man in Ongaia to the large boom poles extending from the hull of the canoe. The rattan, or cane, used is from a forest liana. It is a recalcitrant material so the artisan is using a stone to hammer it into suppliance. In illustration 148, one of the supports has been lashed to it, a more efficient and customary technique which gives the flexibility needed to give with the motions of the sea.

149–150   *The launching*
This party is shoving off from the beach at Kurvok with a new canoe decorated with plants along its gunwales and the crew in a festive mood. The canoe went round the other Kilenge villages of Waremo, Ulumaiinge and Ongaia to solicit presents.

The canoe *singsing* is over. The party has returned to Kurvok and gone ashore. It has entrusted the dismantling of the mast and the anchoring of the new canoe to the small boy on the platform.

151   *Attachment of platform to hull*
This photograph was taken lying on the ground and looking up at the underside of the platform of the canoe in order to illustrate how the platform is attached to a frame, which, in turn, has been lashed across the length of the hull.

153   *Kilenge canoe being towed by the Leo*
I had always understood that Kilenge canoes were quite unsuited to being towed by a launch, such as the Leo, the launch of the Catholic mission, Kilenge. The bow of a Siassi canoe is somewhat more rounded and tends to rise up forward more than that of a Kilenge canoe (cf. *ill.* 183). I have seen a Siassi canoe towed for a couple of hours behind a launch off Umboi Island and also seen one towed by the Leo to Cape Gloucester. Off Kandoka, once, the Leo tried to tow a Kaliai canoe, which is similar to that of the Kilenge, with disastrous results. The Kilenge canoe in this illustration was picked up off Sag-sag by the Leo, having asked for a tow back to Tawale, from whence it originated, after a trip south in search of trochus shells. The tow rope was attached to the bow and broke once after we had got under way, but it had a stout line from the bow to the outrigger to keep the outrigger rigidly parallel to the hull of the canoe so that it didn't splay out as the launch went ahead. The device was successful and the tow made passage astern at some eight or nine knots without plowing its bow under. The two men facing aft are happily trolling for Spanish mackerel.

154   *Fishing nets drying in Kurvok*
Fishing nets used in the big fishing drive on the reefs south of Ongaia are shown drying. The sinkers are generally small clam shells. The floats are of two principal kinds: a small square one which is distinguished as the female float and a long one which is referred to as a male float. The former predominate and are painted (cf. *ill.* 155); the latter are usually carved only (cf. *ill.* 157) but sometimes, as can be seen in the centre of this illustration, are painted.

155   *Fishing nets in Ongaia*

156   *Kilenge canoe from Tawale at Ongaia*
This canoe is making passage to Cape Gloucester for a *singsing*. It has paused at Ongaia beach on the way. The sail is about to be set after they have shoved off.

157   *Net floats in Waremo*
Three well carved net floats, which the Kilenge distinguish as male floats, are shown (cf. *ills.* 159–160).

158, 163–164   AGOSANG *dancers with shield and spear*
The dance *agosang* consists of long passages of women in pairs or lines placed in a half circle (*ills.* 168–169), dancing back and forth towards the central chorus of men which consists of drummers and dancers with shields and spears. The dancers stand 'protectively' in front of the drummers. Every now and again the men make a 'sortie' (*ills.* 158, 163), turn (*ill.* 164) and retreat back to the drummers followed by the women. The dance in one aspect seems to symbolize a sense of opposition between the sexes. The actions of the women are almost taunting, or tempting, as they dance provocatively towards the men, who in their turn 'drive' them away, though only in a formalized manner, not realistically threatening them. In former times *agosang* might be the occasion for

a set-to at the end of the dance between men of opposing factions in order to pay back some debt, a murder or a rape, by spearing the suspected culprit or one of his kinsmen.

159–160 *Net floats, Lambe village, Garove Island*

Some of the net floats seen on Garove Island, which is the largest of the Vitu Islands, are beautifully carved. That shown in illustration 160 is painted too. The mask form is of particular interest: the design is the same as that of an actual mask seen on Garove Island and shows the continuation of a style which was present before the first world war (see *ill.* 95). The Lambe villagers did not make the sex distinction of the floats as the Kilenge did. The sinkers were largely cowrie shells and stones.

161 *Canoe transporting clay pots*

This canoe had been to Sag-sag to trade. There it had obtained the clay pots seen strung from a pole, which was attached to the edge of the canoe platform. The pots originated from Sio Island, off the northern shores of the Huon Peninsula, from whence they had been traded to the Siassis, and from there across the Dampier Strait to Sag-sag. The traders, who had paused for the night at Kilenge, were on their way back to Talasea, the Kilenge said, meaning that they were Kombei.

162 *Trading voyage*

Another of the fleet of canoes which had been to Sag-sag to trade paused for the night at Kilenge. Part of the canoe transporting the pots which was pictured in the previous illustration can be seen in the top left hand section of the photograph. The shields the visitors bring with them are carried when they dance for their hosts or sometimes are traded to them, for the Kilenge no longer make shields and rely on obtaining them from the east where they are still made.

165 AGOSANG *dancer with boar's tusks*

Each dancer who carries a shield and spear wears an ornament of two boar's tusks which are attached to a cord and hang from his neck on his chest. When he makes a sortie he grips the ornament in his teeth. Attached to this ornament and looking rather like shredded paper are some leaves which have been teased out and dyed purple, green and yellow. At the top of his forehead is an ornament of bright coloured leaves.

166 *Learning to dance*

Little girls are dressed up for *singsings* from a very early age and soon learn to imitate the steps of their elders.

167 *Women resting at a* SINGSING

The dance skirt of the Kilenge is very heavy and a rest is needed from time to time, for a *singsing* will often go on all night till dawn, having started up soon after sunset.

168 *Women dancing at* AGOSANG

See notes to illustration 158.

169 SIA *in Ulumaiinge*

A round of *Sia* has just got underway in Ulumaiinge. It started in the late afternoon, specially early so that I could photograph it. It continued on and off for two days and nights. It was part of a cycle of *singsings* which was sponsored by Talania of Ulumaiinge. The taro crop was poor and he was unable to finish the cycle started the year before, nor was he able to finish it while we were staying in Kilenge. The Kilenge say they got *Sia* from the Siassis and it is possible that it originated on the mainland in the Huon Peninsula area. It was certainly well established in West New Britain before the first world war, as early photographs bear witness, and also existed on the mainland before the turn of the century, as one or two specimens in museums testify. *Sia* is, in some ways, the most interesting of the Kilenge *singsings* and certainly the most dramatic. For while in the other *singsings* most of the dancing is done by the women, the dancing is rather formalized and limiting to the performer. In *Sia* there is considerable individual expression in a round (*e.g. ill.* 177) and great freedom for individual expression in many of the dances whether by the leader of a round (*e.g. ills.* 171, 173, 175), a solo dancer (*e.g. ill.* 176) or in group performances or duets.

170 *Women costumed for the* SINGSING

As part of a woman's decoration for *singsing*, a considerable variety of leaves of plants are stuck into the back of their dance skirts, into their armbands and hung around the neck. These last are generally sweet smelling or sometimes pleasantly pungent, depending on the person's preference in perfumes.

171 *Talania of Ulumaiinge leading a chorus of* SIA *in Ulumaiinge*

In the background can be seen two women costumed for the *singsing*. They only dance on the side-lines at *Sia*.

172 *A new chorus at* SIA *starts up*

Cf. *ill.* 178 for bag of dog's teeth worn as part of costume of dancer in foreground. Here, and in illustrations 173–174, 176 and 178, *Sia* was performed at Malangon.

173 *Talania of Ulumaiinge*

Talania loved *Sia* and danced it with great verve, as can be seen from this photograph. He is about to strike the hour-glass drum he holds in his left hand.

174 *Sakaiil of Waremo costumed for* SIA

Sakaiil, like Talania of neighbouring Ulumaiinge, was a lover of *Sia*. Here he is shown taking a brief rest. The borders of his hat are made of paper. In days of yore they would have been of white feathers. Some traditionalists still use feathers as can be seen in illustration 172. Resting on his chest with some sweet smelling leaves are two boars tusks which hang from around his neck. His headband is of dog's teeth and nassa shells.

175 *Sakaiil of Waremo leading a chorus of* SIA

176 SIA *dancer imitating* SAUMOY

The solo dancer is shown imitating the movements of

saumoy, the fishing eagle, which can sometimes be seen soaring majestically high up the mountain over the forest or, at others, gliding towards the sea and then pausing, almost as though still, on a counter current of air before resuming his swing along the coast and examination of the waters below.

177 SIA *dancer*
This dancer is one of the chorus in the middle of a round of *Sia*.

178 *Navona of Waremo resting*
Navona is the 'Big Man' of Waremo. Here he is rolling a cigarette for a smoke in an interval in the performance of *Sia*. Over his left hip is a fine net bag decorated with dog's teeth. Some of the decorative plants worn by dancers at *singsings* are shown clearly in the photograph. Mostly they are grown specifically for the purpose.

179 *Stern of Kaliai canoe*
Painting on the stern of Penga of Kandoka's canoe which had paused at Ongaia on its way home from trading at Sag-sag. The design and arrangement of the forms seemed to fall into the Kilenge pattern of designing but the Kilenge were not able to name the motifs present.

180–181 *Siassi canoe at Kurvok*
This type of canoe, which is made by the Siassi neighbours of the Kilenge, is in striking contrast to the local outrigger canoe. The Siassi canoe has the hull built up on each side, thus providing a hold for cargo additional to that carried on the outrigger platform (see next illustration). Extended sides, or washstrakes, also reduce the shipping of water when any sort of sea is running, an important factor when sailing in the turbulent waters of the Dampier and Vitiaz Straits. This particular canoe was made on the island of Tuam though it belonged to a Mandok islander. In the background is Sakar Island.

This is the same canoe as in the previous illustration. It is shown being loaded a few hours before its departure. It had been at Kilenge for several weeks, having brought one or two women for care at the mission hospital as well as to trade. It also brought a Mandok carver and one or two relatives of the Kilenge for a visit. It brought over in its cargo some carved wooden bowls, essential items in the bride price (see *ills.* 213–232). Among its returning cargo were a considerable variety of vegetable foods, including sweet potatoes, bananas and *pitpit*, a wild form of sugar cane, and locally grown tobacco for which the Kilenge are well known. The canoe's outrigger is not visible in the illustration, being behind the house beams on the left.

182 *Setting sails for departure*
The sails of the canoe depicted in the previous two illustrations have been hoisted and are being adjusted before the canoe is shoved off from the beach and poled across the shallows of the reef seaward until it catches the easterly wind, which will help it return across the Dampier Strait. The photograph is an important record of the traditional use of plaited matting sails. They contrast with those used by the Kilenge (cf. *ill.* 156) who use imported cloth, if available.

183 *Mandok Por as seen from Mandok Island*
The very small island of Mandok Por with the Catholic mission station and school house can be seen in the distance. Beyond is the coastline of Umboi Island. In the foreground are canoes drawn up on the beach of Mandok Island.

184 *Canoe prow and stern, Mandok Por*
The illustration shows the carved prow and stern of two canoes on the beach of Mandok Por. The carving in the foreground is of a sea eagle clutching a flying fish (cf. *ill.* 185).

185 *Canoe prow, Ongaia village*
The same motif appearing in the previous illustration is shown here freshly carved by Gwau of Ongaia village, Kilenge, a man in his forties. Gwau's grandfather was a Kilenge man. When a lad, his father was sent to Mandok to a family, who, in turn, sent a son to live with Gwau's father's family in Kilenge. In due course, Gwau was sent by his father from Mandok to live with his grandfather's family in Ongaia. Gwau had been brought up on Mandok long enough to absorb the Mandok style.

186 *Stern of Mandok canoe*
The canoe is drawn up on the beach at Mandok Por. The design is comparable to that shown in illustration 184.

187 *Adzing a canoe, Mandok Island*
The artist is depicted finishing the side of a canoe with an adze. The canoe is a small one and has a single plank attached either side to the hull to extend the sides upward in contrast to the double strakes building up the sides of the large sea-going canoe shown in illustration 180.

188 *Mandok paddles*
The photograph of paddles on Mandok Island shows the carving executed where the stem and back of the paddles meet. The construction of the designs on all three are basically similar. That on the left is the most elaborately executed and provides one with a key to the import of the other two, for it clearly illustrates the form of a mask with markings above and below the eyes in which a snake form is carved. The design would seem to represent a theme encountered before and a widespread one, namely, the depiction of *nausung* and a snake, thus referring to the two brothers, one of whom had the body of a snake. The design was noted, for example, as present sometimes on turtle shell armlets (*e.g. ill.* 40) or coconuts (*e.g. ill.* 190), or on drums (*e.g. ills.* 101, 107), or on hooks (*ills.* 209–212); it seems to have quite a wide range of expression and appears with considerable variation of detail, but always around the two basic motifs of eye forms and a snake's body.

189–190 *Carved coconuts from Huon Gulf*

These two coconuts are from a large collection in the Rautenstrauch-Joest Museum which originates from the Tami Islands and the coast of the Huon Peninsula. That in illustration 190 shows clearly the mask form referred to in the previous illustration; that in illustration 189 shows the snake and a very abstract version of the mask.

191 *Sideboard of Mandok canoe*

Shown is the carved board of a small canoe on Mandok Island which is attached to the side of the platform, the side opposite the outrigger. The motif represented in the projections carved on either side of the board is the fishing eagle clutching a flying fish. This was noted in illustrations 184–185.

192 *Two carved coconuts of the Kilenge*

That on the left, which is 10.5 cms. high and has a maximum opening of 8.5 cms., was carved by Nongi of Kurvok in 1967. The other, on the right, which is 11 cms. high and has a maximum opening of 10.5 cms., was carved by Marakos of Ongaia, who died in 1965.

193 *Carved coconut from Tami Islands*

This carved coconut, which is Number 868–851 in the collection of the Rijksmuseum voor Volkenkunde, Leiden, is 9.5 cms. high and has a maximum opening of 15 cms. It is recorded as being from the Tami Islands but was collected quite a long while ago, the Rijksmuseum having acquired it from Dr. Otto Schellong in 1888. The design is similar to that on the Kilenge coconut on the right in the next illustration.

194–197 *Canoe bailer*

This bailer, which is 37.3 cms. long and 11 cms. wide, was carved by Talania of Ongaia in 1966. Mooro is represented by the human face carved at the end (*ill.* 194) and the snake, which is on the handle (*ill.* 195). The handle also depicts a bird's head, that of *saumoy*, the sea eagle.

198 *Tami canoe bailer (Wuppertal)*

This bailer, which is approximately 46 cms. long, is from the Tami Islands. The snake and sea-eagle are represented as in the next specimen (cf. 199–200).

199–200 *Two Taro spoons and dish from the Tami Islands (Wuppertal)*

From left to right, respectively, the lengths of the specimens, in cms., are approximately 70, 53.5 and 67. Both the taro spoons have present the mask theme associated among the Kilenge with *nausung*, carved where the handle and the scoop meet (cf. *ills.* 86–94). The handle of the spoon in the centre has been broken off. The dish in the form of a fish relates to the bowl complex in which carved wooden bowls are used as food dishes. But this particular dish is rather small and may have been used for a particular food in the display of food in carved bowls (cf. *ills.* 213–232).

201–204 *Two 'modern' Tami taro spoons*

The spoons in illustrations 201–202 is 60 cms. long and that in illustrations 203–204 is 68.5 cms. in length. The spoons were bought from a shop in Lae, New Guinea. The man and snake motif, which is associated with Mooro in Kilenge culture, is apparent in the carved figure at the join of the handle and scoop in each spoon. The same motif, though somewhat differently represented, is to be noted on the side of the Mandok bowl in illustration 222. The figure is also to be compared with those on the neck rest in illustrations 205–208, a Tami carving, and on the Kilenge bowl in illustrations 225–228.

205–208 *Two carved neck rests from the Tami Islands (Wuppertal)*

The neck rest composed of two figures back to back is 17 cms. high, approximately. The two figures may be representative of the two culture heroes which the Kilenge call Mooro and Aisipel, but there is no apparent snake symbol on the carving. The Tami islanders produced a large number of neck rests and the representation of two figures back to back is quite common. In fact, janus motifs occur not only in Tami art but among the Kilenge too.

The bird, which is the main form of the other neck rest, may be a representation of the sandpiper.

209–212 *Tami carved hook (Wuppertal)*

The carved wooden hook is approximately 43.5 cms. in length. The snake and head motif encountered on other objects and in Kilenge art is clearly delineated here in almost full relief down the main stem of this very finely carved hook and is also repeated, in very low relief, on the shoulders of the person represented. Hooks like this were used to suspend various articles under the roof of a house. The hook is, of course, placed upside down in the illustrations.

213 *Roughing out the shape of a bowl*

Using an iron axe, this Mandok carver is roughing out the shape of a wooden bowl which has been for so long in the area a very important item of the bride price. The Tami islanders used to have a monopoly on bowl carving which gradually was taken over by the Siassi islanders in the twenties. Tami, or now, Siassi bowls were traded west into Astrolabe Bay and east as far as the Vitu Islands. The wood is referred to as *kwila*, a Melanesian Pidgin term for either *Afzalea* or *Instia bijuga*, an ironwood tree.

214–215 *Carving a bowl, Mandok*

These two illustrations show a Mandok carver working with a knife on the centre motif on the side of a wooden bowl. The wood at this stage is an orangy colour, which is quite a brilliant colour when the wood is just being cut, as in the previous illustration. The design in front of the carver's right elbow represents a crocodile and snake.

216–217 *Enhancing the carved designs on a bowl, Mandok*

Marimbu, a Mandok artist, who carved this bowl, has blackened it using old torch batteries to obtain the black colouring matter and a pig's tusk with which to polish it. He then rubbed a paste of coral lime over the area of incision and low relief carving (*ill.* 216). He let the paste dry for a short while and then wiped it off, leaving the carved design on the side suitably enhanced. The two main motifs of the design are somewhat differently placed on the side of the bowl from the manner noted on the bowl in illustrations 214–215. The bowl is 65 cms. in length.

218–222 *Carved bowl from Mandok Island.* (1964).

This bowl, which measures 81 cms. in length and is 18 cms. deep at the centre, combines the snake and crocodile forms somewhat differently from the manner in which they were employed in the previous two speci-mens (*ills.* 214–217). The snake reaches to the figure of a person in illustrations 219 and 222, recalling, for example, the Tami wooden hook (*ills.* 209–212); it is combined, on either side of the bowl (*ills.* 218–220), with a form which is different from the crocodile noted on the previous bowl (*ills.* 216–217) and which is, in fact, different in both cases; the crocodile noted in illustrations 214–217, however, appears in janus forms on the bottom of the bowl and the snake is indicated by two 'wiggles' in the spinal column (*ill.* 221). The person represented by the human figure was said to be a man called Nguam, who came from the Tami Islands.

223–224 *Carved Tami bowl*

This bowl was obtained in Lae and it was assumed to be Tami work. It may well be an old piece, for the uncarved surfaces of the inside and outside appear to have been scraped and the whole cleaned up. The colour of the undecorated areas is that of the natural wood. At the front of the bowl is represented the sea-eagle with a flying fish in its beak (*ill.* 224). On either side of the bar joining the bird and fish is a snake motif, which is repeated on the right side only of the ruff of the neck of the bird. The bowl rests on two feet which are shaped in the form of a fish. Between them and the bird's head, on its chest, is a form which may represent a crocodile. The bowl is 60.5 cms. long and 17 cms. wide.

225–228 *Carved Kilenge bowl*

This bowl, which is 61 cms. long, was carved by Makele of Ongaia quite a while before these photographs were taken of it. It demonstrates clearly that the Kilenge were perfectly capable of carving a bowl as good as any carved from Tami or the Siassis but, because of the monopoly of those two places, did not in ordinary practice do so. This is the only example I know of a Kilenge-made bowl of the Tami type. Makele said that the human figure was a representation of *nausung ambam*, which he obtained from his mother. The marks on the limbs of the figure represent its bones (*ills.* 226 and 228). The motif held by each hand is not meant to be anything special, just a flower. The forms on either side of the figure (*ills.* 225–227) do not represent a fish but just a motif that he had at the back of his mind.

There is no indication of the presence of any form of a snake.

229–230 *Tami bowl* (*Neuendettelsau*)

This carved bowl from Tami, which is broken slightly at one end, is 51 cms. long. The designs on the sides are unusual though include the snake. Bodrogi (1961: 99–100), in his authoritative consideration of the earlier data on Huon Gulf art, notes that the 'shining black' of the bowls 'is obtained by rubbing in soil with a manganese or graphite content. This material comes from the islands of Umboi and Lagaueng' and was mixed 'with the sap of the root of the beech almond' before being applied. Bodrogi (*ibid.*) also noted that the wooden bowls were 'carved almost exclusively from the wood of the *Afzelia biyuga*.'

231–232 *Tami bowl*

This bowl was obtained in Lae and was said to be modern Tami work. It is 55 cms. long, 29 cms. wide and 10 cms. deep. The head of the sea-eagle and the wings, folded along the side, and tail feathers, are features comparable to those seen on the bowl in illustrations 223–224. But there the eagle is shown with a fish in its beak. Here the fish has been reduced to incised lines on the bottom of the bowl. A small oval mark, to be seen near the tail on this bowl, or marks very similar to it, is often found on the bottom of the bowls and may be the artist's 'mark'. This seems more likely on this bowl than it representing the anus of the bird.

233 *House post with artist, Mandok*

Mr. Aibale of Mandok is shown beside the house post which he said he had carved when much younger. The manner in which the tongue sticks out is similar to the way in which the Kilenge depict it (see *ills.* 82 and 89) but the mouth seems a compromise between a Kilenge and Tami version (cf. 82, 89, 90). The eye marks are close to those on the Tami house post shown in the next two illustrations, or on the Tami mask in illustration 90. The post was one of four main posts supporting a house. One of the other three had been roughly shaped in preparation for carving a human face as shown here but the other two were plain (cf. *ill.* 238).

234–235 *House post, Tami Islands* (*Cologne*)

This carved house post, which was on exhibition in the Rautenstrauch-Joest Museum (No. 44674), was formerly in the collections of the Museum für Völkerkunde, Berlin. It was obtained from the Tami Islands. The post measures 169 cms. in height, 31.5 cms. in width and 27 cms. thick.

236 *Model house, Tami Islands* (*Neuendettelsau*)

There are a number of model houses in museum col-lections which are indicative of earlier Tami style houses, though one cannot be certain how accurately they represent either a men's house or a dwelling. House posts comparable to those depicted here are to be noted in illustrations 233–235, 238–240. Both on Umboi Island, in the Siassis and on the Tami Islands the practice was to use hewn planks as walls rather than plaited or woven screens of bamboos. The Kombei on Tamuniai Island also use plank walls (*ill.* 242). The planks provided the carver with an opportunity for carving, or the painter for painting, too apparent to miss. How far ordinary homes had their side walls decorated with carved planks is not certain, but men's houses were probably always suitably embellished. The carving represented on this plank is particularly intriguing as it combines, in a compact design —the Tami 'form'—a number of motifs representative of themes basic to the area with which the Tami islanders had contact. The design combines the crocodile, the mask form associated with *nausung* among the Kilenge, and the snake (cf. *ill.* 243). Among the Tami islanders the crocodile seems to have been associated with initiation of boys into manhood. This association the Kilenge never made, so they say today. A masked figure appeared at 'initiation', taking this to be, at minimum, circumcision. The presence of a snake form, shown on the design on the plank as the first part of the crocodile's spinal column, together with the eyes of a 'mask', or human, seem to indicate that the equivalent of the Kilenge Mooro is meant to be represented. The crocodile is shown with a dog in its jaws, a symbolic representation, perhaps, of the consuming of the uninitiated boy, later to be returned to society as a man, and, at another level, and perhaps at an earlier point in time, the whole design was meant to symbolize what we would term a cannibalistic act. The borders of the plank represent the form of a snake.

237 *Kilenge carved pole, Nekarop Village*

Nekarop is a village to the west of Silimate. This pole, which is about 2.75 metres high, was commissioned by Markis of Silimate and Liluluage of Nekarop in 1965 and carved by Viriu of Garamati and Mosokai of Silimate with Markis' *nausung*, Talawagi. Such a pole is erected now sometimes to mark the occasion of circumcision or to honour the oldest daughter and mark her coming of age.

238 *House post, Silimate Village*

This house post, which is janus in form, unlike those in the previous illustration, was commissioned by Tundua of Silimate village, a Kilenge village not far from Bariai country to the east. The people of Silimate are only recently settled on the coast, after the second world war. The post was carved by Viriu of Garamati, a village neighbouring Silimate. Tundua had it made to honour his daughter Angeta when she was about eleven years old.

239–240 *House for seclusion of young girl, Tamuniai Island*

Tamuniai is an island off the Bariai coast inhabited by Kombei people. A house on carved and painted posts

was erected to honour a young girl called Galiki where she was secluded for a period, not being allowed to come out of the house, except at night, some said. According to the Kilenge, a Kombei girl would be secluded in a house such as this one for a month until, one night, a *singsing* was held in her honour and she returned to the village. On the right hand post (*ill.* 239) is depicted Aisipel. He is depicted again on the left hand one but with his brother Mooro on the back (*ill.* 240). The snake is clearly shown on the latter. The jaws of a snake are carved at the top of the post which provides a support for one of the main beams of the small house.

241 *Kilenge 'mobile' at the end of a house beam, Nekarop Village*

This 'mobile', or *natalakaringa* as the Kilenge call it, was carved out of the end of the main beam which forms the front support of the house and hangs down from it, as shown here. The house belongs to Bele of Nekarop. The 'mobile', which in this case is janus in form, generally represents the owner's personal mark (see *ills.* 40–47).

242 *Painted plank wall of house, Tamuniai Island*

Some houses on Tamuniai Island had painted plank walls, such as this one; others had screens of plaited split bamboo, as can be seen in illustration 212. The painted designs seem to represent a different tradition of forms and motifs to those encountered on the Tami and Mandok carvings illustrated previously.

243 *Painted wall of men's house, Lama Village, Garove Island*

Two major motifs noted in illustration 236 as combined in an integrated design on the plank wall of a Tami model house are here separately represented: the eyes of the mask and the markings above and below the eye are painted on the wall of the men's house in red, green, white and black colours; the crocodile is carved and can be seen sticking out of the front of the house under the gable. Garove Island, one of the Vitu Islands, represents the easternmost point of Tami influence in former times. The Kilenge used to trade with them.

244–245 *Kilenge 'mobile' ornament*

This *natalakaringa* was carved by Namongo of Ongaia in July, 1966. It was given to my wife and myself to keep in our house at Kilenge to bring us good luck. It represented our personal crest. Such an object was put on top of a house, I was told, but I never saw one. It is made out of three pieces of wood and the designs are painted on. A wooden peg, which fits into the base, penetrates the centre arm and protrudes up into the top piece. The two top pieces can each pivot. The longer one is 42 cms. in length. The height of the object is 28 cms.

1　*Village of Ulumaiinge with Mount Talawe behind*　　　2　*Approach to the village of Ongaia from the east*

3 *Entrance to Kilenge from the west*

4 *Kurvok and Portne villages at dawn*   **5** *View of* HAUS PLIS, *copra shed and cooperative store*

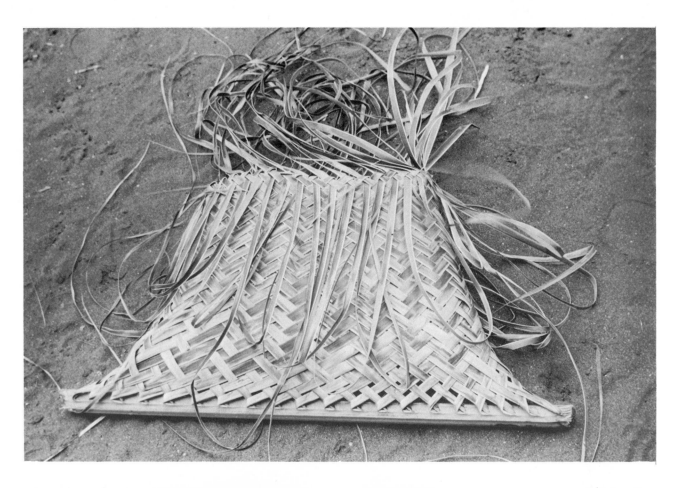

6–8 *Woman making a handbag*

9–10 *Marakos of Ongaia making a basket*

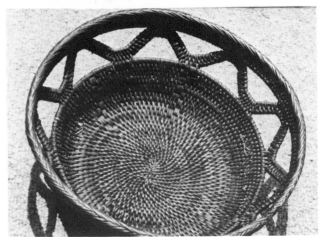
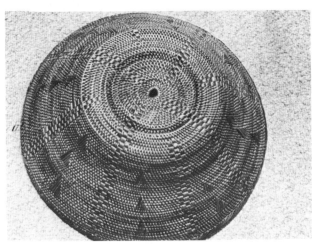
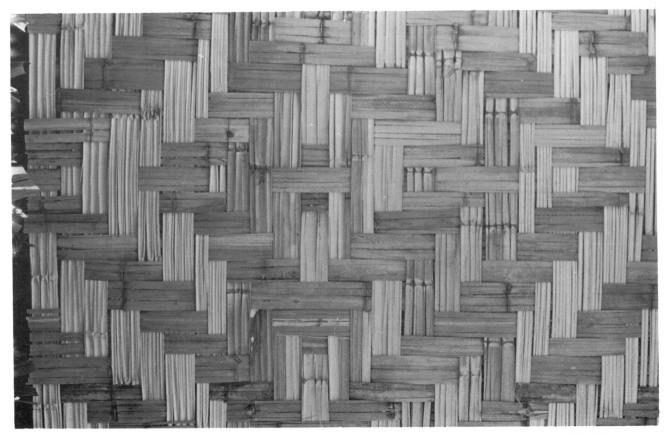

11–14 *Basket-making in the Kilenge* LOLO   **15** *House screen*

16 *Building a new* HAUS KIAP *at Kilenge*   17 *Putting the finishing touches to a new house in Kurvok*

18 *Squaring off floor beams of a new house in Kurvok*

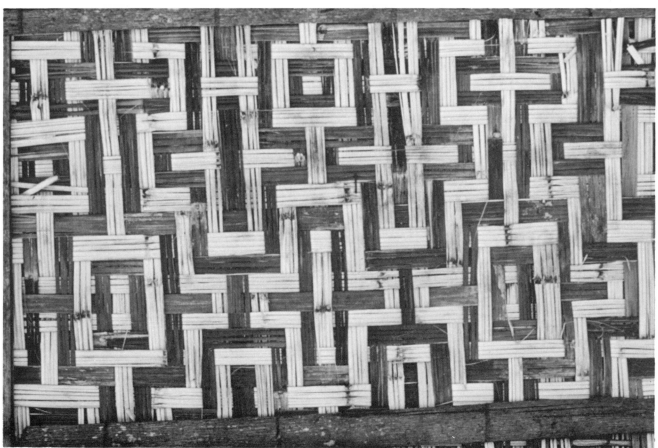

19–21 *Making a house screen*

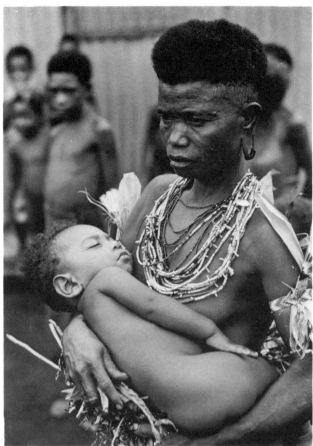

22 *Maleu of Kilenge with a headband of dog's teeth*

23 *Donga of Ulumaiinge with her grandchild*

24 *Aisapo of Ongaia*

25 *Makele of Ongaia*

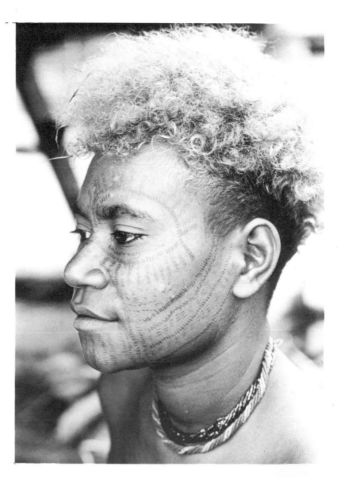

26–27 *Mundua of Portne*

28–29 *Akisa of Portne*

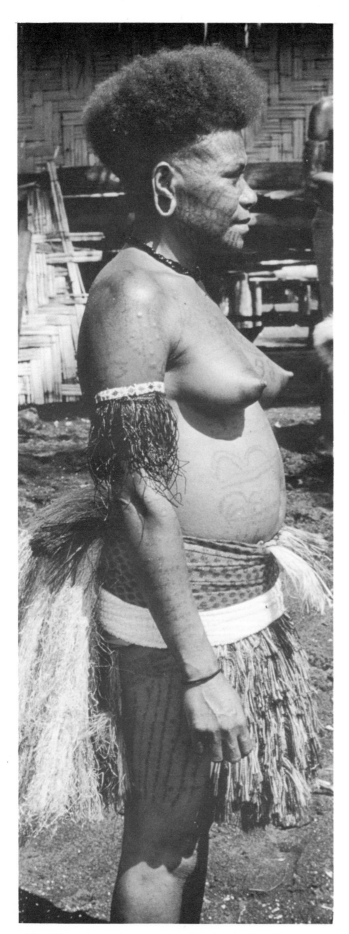

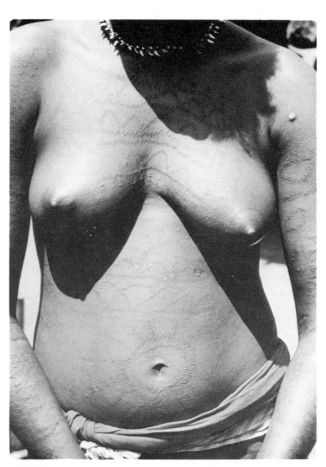

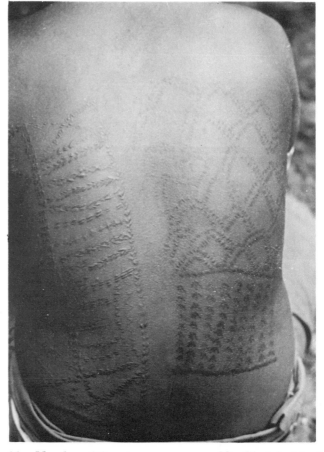

30 *Luguvia of Portne costuming for a* SINGSING   **31** *Mundua of Ongaia*   **32** *Cicatrized back*

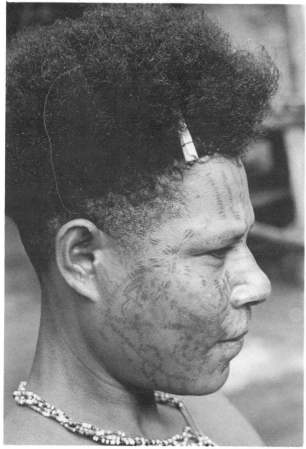

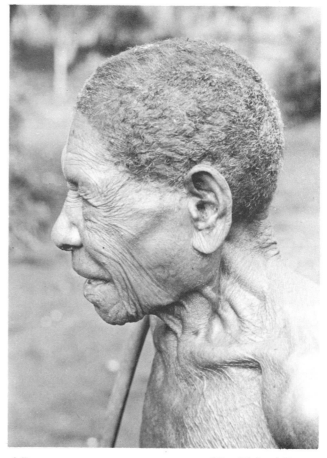

33 *Making a shell bracelet*   **34** *Giarop of Portne*   **35** *Tiele of Portne*

61

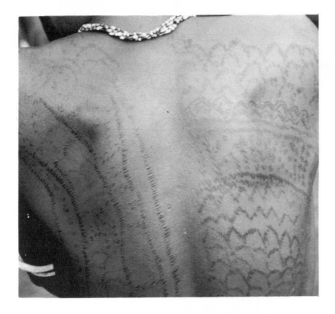

36 *Cicatrized back* **37–39** *Making shell bracelets* **40–43** *Kilenge and Mandok turtle shell armlets*

44–54 *Kilenge turtle shell armlets*

55   *Kilenge turtle shell arm-rings*   **56**   *Kilenge armbands*   **57–58**   *Preparing a dance skirt*

59 *Preparing a dance skirt*

60 *Donga of Ulumaiinge in dance skirt*

61 *Woman of Kurvok in dance skirt*

62 *The village of Ongaia*　　　　　　　　**63** *Clearing the bush for a garden*

64 NATAPTAVO *mask*

65 NATAPTAVO *masks dancing at a* SINGSING

66 WAGILI *masquerader resting*   67 NATAPTAVO *mask and cloak*   68 NATAPTAVO *masqueraders in Portne*

69 NATAPTAVO *masqueraders at Cape Gloucester*   70   *Masqueraders costuming at Birik, Umboi Island*

71–72 *Masqueraders, Umboi Island*

73 SINGSING *begins at Birik, Umboi Island*

74 *Mask on Tamuniai Island*   **75** *Masquerader at Cape Gloucester*   **76–77** NAUSUNG *dancing at Malangon*

78—81 *Talania of Ongaia, master artist, carving a* NAUSUNG *mask*

82 *Painted* NAUSUNG *mask*

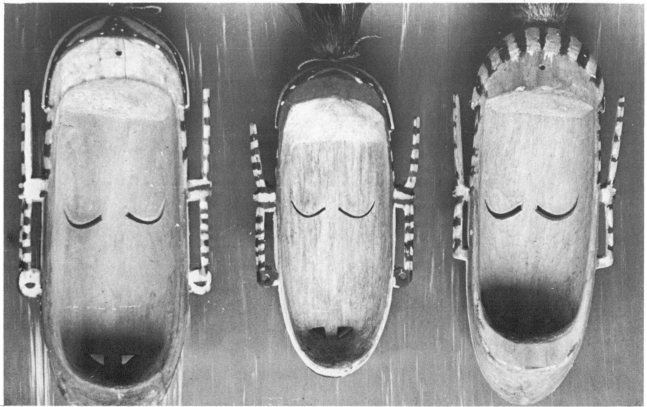

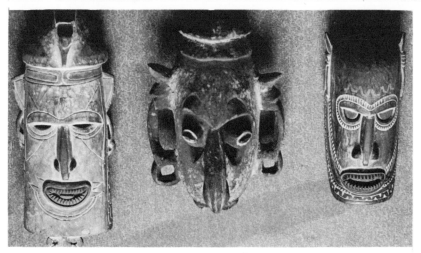

83–87 NAUSUNG *masks*

88 NAUSUNG *masks*

89–90 *Tami-style masks*

91 *Mask from Umboi Island*

92–93 *Kilenge (?) mask*   **94** *Rai Coast mask*   **95** *Mask from the Vitu Islands*

96 *Tami* TAGO *mask*

97 *Tami* TAGO *mask*

98 *Tami* TAGO *masks*

99 *Talania of Ongaia adzing a drum*

100–102 *Drums*

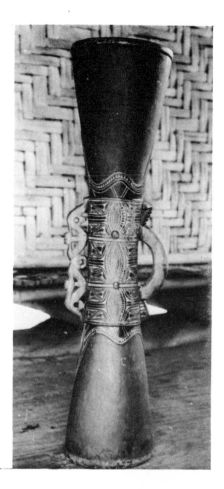

103–105 – *Drum*

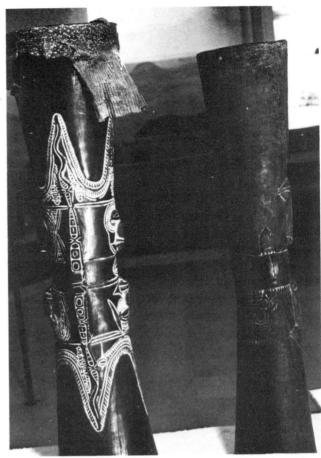

107–109 *Two Tami drums*

110 *Siassi drum*

111   BUKUMO *being constructed in Portne*   112   BUKUMO *dancing in Portne*

113 BUKUMO *being constructed in Kurvok*

114–115 *Nake of Portne drawing mask designs*

116–117 *Canoe designs*

118–120 NAUSUNG *designs*   **121** NATAPTAVO *mask design*   **122** *Canoe design*

123–126 NATAPTAVO *mask designs*

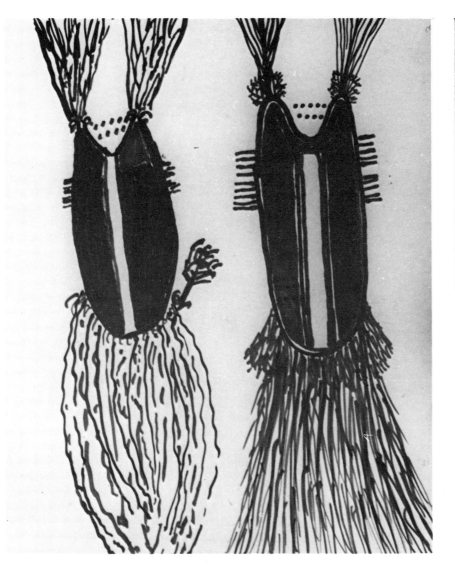

127 NATAPTAVO *mask design*

128–130 *Kilenge dance clubs*

131 *Two canoes in Ongaia*   132 *Stern of large canoe*

133–134 *Bow of large canoe*

135 *Stern of Bariai canoe*

136–137 *Stern of large canoe*

138–139 *Small canoe*

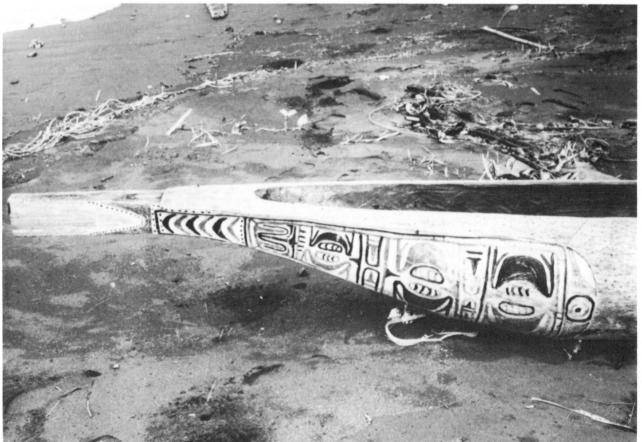

140–141 *Small canoe*

142–144 *Adzing and painting hull of new canoe*

145 *Painting a canoe*

146–148 *Renewing the lashings*

149–150 *The launching*   **151** *Attachment of platform to hull*   **152** *Painting*   **153** *Kilenge canoe being towed by the Leo*

154 *Fishing nets drying in Kurvok*

155 *Fishing nets in Ongaia*

156 *Kilenge canoe from Tawale at Ongaia*

157   *Net floats in Waremo*

158   AGOSANG *dancers with shield and spear*

159–160   *Net floats, Lambe village, Garove Island*

161 *Canoe transporting clay pots*   162 *Trading voyage*

163–164 AGOSANG *dancers*

165 AGOSANG *dancer with boar's tusks*

166 *Learning to dance*

167 *Women resting at a* SINGSING

168 *Women dancing at* AGOSANG

169 SIA *in Ulumaiinge*

170 *Women costumed for the* SINGSING

109

171 *Talania of Ulumaiinge leading a chorus*

172 *A new chorus at* SIA *starts up*

173 *Talania of Ulumaiinge*

174 *Sakaiil of Waremo costumed for* SIA

175 *Sakaiil of Waremo leading a chorus*

176 *Dancer imitating* SAUMOY

177 SIA *dancer*   **178** *Navona of Waremo resting*   **179** *Stern of Kaliai canoe*

180–181 *Siassi canoe at Kurvok*

182 *Setting sails for departure*   183 *Mandok Por as seen from Mandok Island*

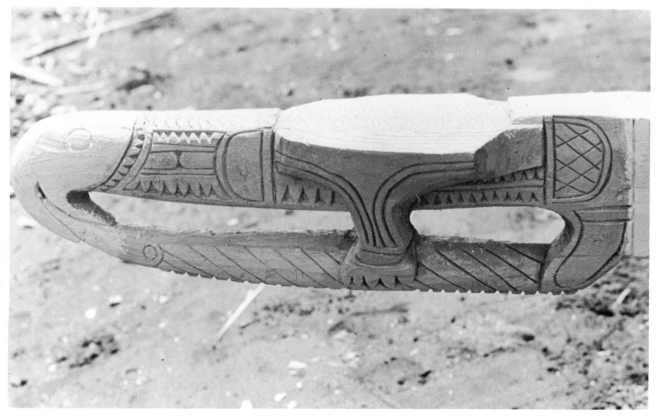

184 *Canoe prow and stern, Mandok Por*   **185** *Canoe prow, Ongaia village*

186 *Stern of Mandok canoe*   **187** *Adzing a canoe*

188 *Mandok paddles*

189–190 *Carved coconuts from Huon Gulf*

191 *Sideboard of Mandok canoe*   **192** *Two carved coconuts of the Kilenge*   **193** *Carved coconut from Tami Islands*

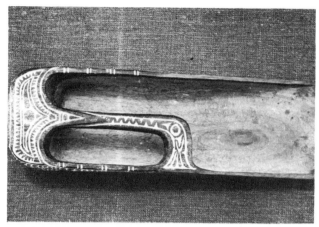
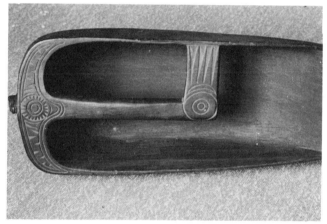
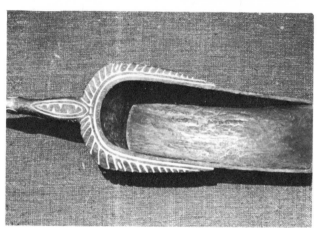
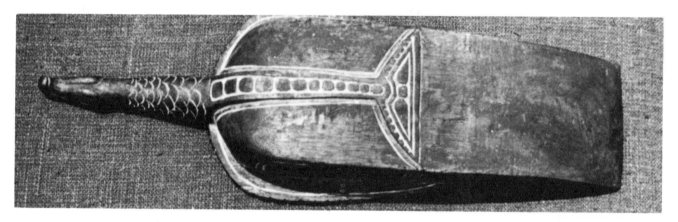
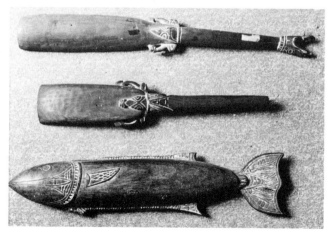
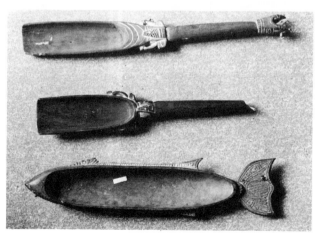

194–198 *Canoe bailers*

199–200 *Two Taro spoons and dish from the Tami Islands*

201–204 *Two 'modern' Tami taro spoons*   **205** *Two carved neck rests from the Tami Islands*

206–208 *Carved neck rests*

209–210 *Tami carved hook*

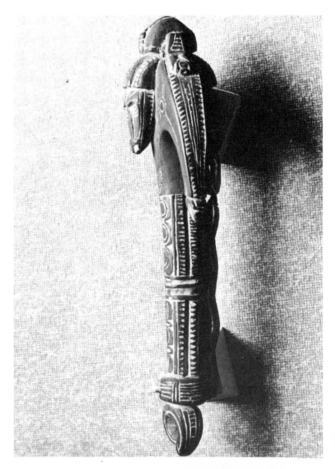

211–212 *Carved hook* **213** *Roughing out the shape of a bowl* **214** *Carving a bowl, Mandok*

215–220 *Carving a bowl, Mandok*

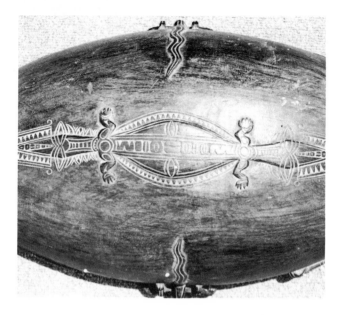

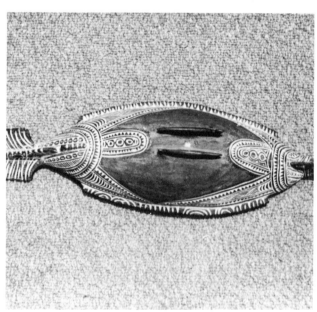

221–222 *Finished bowl*   **223–224** *Carved Tami bowl*   **225–226** *Carved Kilenge bowl*

227–228 *Kilenge bowl* **229–232** *Tami bowls* **233** *House post with artist, Mandok* **234–235** *House post, Tami*

236 *Model house, Tami*   **237** *Carved pole, Nekarop Village*   **238** *House post, Silimate Village*   **239** *Tamuniai house*

240 *Tamuniai house post*   **241** *Kilenge 'mobile'*   **242** *Painted wall of house, Tamuniai Island*

243 *Painted wall of men's house, Lama Village, Garove Island*

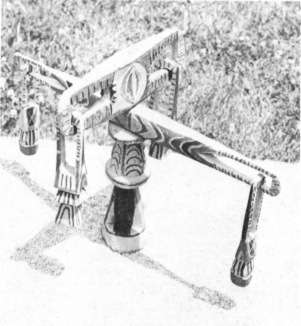

244–245 *Kilenge 'mobile' ornament*